The Vanilla People

(Saga of a Savage family)

By Joie Savage

PublishAmerica
Baltimore

© 2009 by Joie Savage.
All rights reserved. No part of this book may be reproduced, stored in a retrieval system or transmitted in any form or by any means without the prior written permission of the publishers, except by a reviewer who may quote brief passages in a review to be printed in a newspaper, magazine or journal.

First printing

PublishAmerica has allowed this work to remain exactly as the author intended, verbatim, without editorial input.

ISBN: 978-1-61582-003-0 (softcover)
ISBN: 978-1-4489-6805-3 (hardcover)
PUBLISHED BY PUBLISHAMERICA, LLLP
www.publishamerica.com
Baltimore

Printed in the United States of America

This book is dedicated to my grandchildren, Calvin, Cori, and Jane, who will surely not be the last in the vanilla line. Thank you to my lovely cousin Karina for her brain and her inspirations. Thank you to my family for your love and patience. Thank you to Mick, for your never-ending support of this project, and to my editor, Elizabeth Larson, who laughed at all my jokes.

The first half of the book explains Vanilla, the second half tries to apologize. Actually, the second half of the book is a compilation of Twisted Thoughts, a humor column once spread out in a small community newspaper, the Willows Journal. Folks from Willows, California enjoyed the column for several years but in spite of that, they really do have good taste.

Chapter 1
DEFINING VANILLA

Linus once told Lucy, "Five hundred years from now, no one will know the difference." She had told him his drawing of a green giraffe was just plain wrong. I think he may be wrong. If Lucy was saying green giraffes are in bad taste, then 500 years won't make a bit of difference. Bad taste is forever, no matter how you try to escape it.

Herein is the story of the Vanilla People, who epitomize bad taste. Sadly, my family can be Vanilla royalty when it comes to bad taste. I may or may not have developed the Vanilla gene, but I'm definitely a carrier. In my family, there are two flavors of Vanilla, Savage and Whitton.

Vanilla People were given their name because they are the kind of people who take their kids to a 31-flavor ice cream shop and force them to order vanilla, because all other flavors are foreign and therefore evil. French Vanilla, or Freedom Vanilla, and Cherry Vanilla have an evil foreign influence.

If you've never met a Vanilla person, you can easily spot one in the mall. They will be in the food court, wearing something really tacky, and ranting about high prices, between bites. Vanilla folk are big eaters, always talking about food, nearly always hungry. The pictures in their family albums are of people stuffing their faces with meat and potatoes. Their idea of a "night on the town" is going to Denny's. Yes, they are a sight, hungry, angry people in mismatched clothes. This is vanilla. This is my family.

Usually, Vanilla folks are fundamentalist Christians, who will not tolerate different faiths, cultures, or anyone without a southern accent. "Feren" means anything they can't understand or tolerate.

They listen to gospel and country music, because, well, God likes country music. They believe that people who listen to rock and roll are going straight to "h" "e" double toothpicks. If you like opera, you are pretentious, and an ounce of pretension is worth a pound of manure.

Some people have mistaken Vanilla People for trailer trash, or rednecks. It goes deeper than that. Vanilla is to the marrow. It is in the DNA.

Let's establish your Vanilla Quotient (VQ). Here is a list of how you can tell if your family has the Vanilla gene. Answer yes or no...

Is your family coat of arms the Denny's sign?

Have you or any member of your family ever launched the family cat into orbit?

Have you or any member of your family worn something bright orange to a wedding? Would it be a hunting cap with flaps?

Do the older women in your family brag about their bodily functions?

Have you ever felt guilty about eating ice cream that was not Vanilla?

Have you ever experienced anger so intense that you bit something people don't normally bite, such as a wall?

Does your home contain more than one black velvet painting? Is there an Elvis shrine?

Is "Joe" or "Sue" the middle name of most of your relatives?

Are you hungry right now?

Do you abhor literature other than the Bible, TV Guide, or Outdoor Life?

Do you think TV dinners were an amazing invention?

Do you have a watch that features a cat with a mouse second hand, or Christmas ornament jewelry?

Are you threatened by the unknown?

Are you positive God is watching everything you do?

Do you believe someone could jinx you or put a spell on your cat?

Are you extremely fond of butter?

On Halloween, can people tell whether or not you are dressed up?

Do you have a favorite spoon?

Do you still have an 8-track tape deck and a Beta movie player?

Does nearly every member of the family live in the same trailer park?

If the answers to at least two of these questions are yes, your VQ is 25, and you probably have a recessive Vanilla gene.

If you answered yes to 3 to 6 questions, your VQ is 75 and you probably have more than one relative named Dwayne.

If you answered more than 7 questions yes, we are probably related.

My parents were each born with a dominant Vanilla gene. Both Savages and Whittons are ripe with Vanilla beans (crazy vanillans). Mom has giant framed pictures of Jesus and sheep, on black velvet. Mom and Dad don't have a shrine to Elvis, because he didn't sing enough gospel to repent for the rock and roll. He might as well have been the Anti-Christ. When I was a teenager, it was Alice Cooper who was the Evil One. Now we know for sure, the Anti-Christ is really the Taco Bell Chihuahua. After all, he endorses burritos, of all things, and he claims a huge following.

Aunt Elaine (Whitton, married to a Savage) has a photo album of her laundry. I am not making this up. She took pictures of her laundry when she visited a foreign country. She compares them with her photos of her Texas laundry. Same shirt, different city.

These people live near Tyler, Texas in what else, a trailer park. They drive Fords and Chevys. There are two liquor stores nearby, but no one in my family would touch a drop of liquor. It's sinful. The bowling alley is also nearby, and several churches, back in the woods. There are no Starbucks, no institutes of higher learning, no 12-step programs, no Democrats. There are no homes without rifles. There are bugs the size of small aircraft, which are mostly ignored. All the VCRs blink 11.

They didn't always live in a Texas trailer park. The Whittons raised three daughters in a small house in the small town of Sparks, Nevada. But they always had a southern accent and there always seemed to be the scent of Vanilla and a tinge of fresh blood, and never a need for technological advances beyond 1950.

In fact, Dad thinks you have to be quiet when you record a movie. Forget trying to leave a message on their answering machine. They started out with, "You have reached Joyce and Bill. Oh, dad-blame it the little light is blinking. I don't know if I'm talking into the right end of this thing...(muffled sound) and we'll call you back, directly. Hey, Bill do you want to say somethin' into this here machine?" "No." Beep.

Now they have a computer. Mom (a Savage who married a Whitton) has knitted a computer cozy to keep it warm at night. Dad doesn't touch it. If he did, he would keep pushing the control button, trying to get some. If it breaks down, his method of repair would be a shotgun.

Or more likely, he would have the comfort of other Texas relatives standing around looking at it, as if it were a truck engine. "I think it's the catalytic converter, Bill."

"Might be outta gas."

"Did y'all press the escape key and let something outta there?"

As of this writing, my parents have been married nearly 53 years, surprising, given their temperaments. At the celebration of their Golden Wedding Anniversary, people kept saying, "Wow, you've been together 50 years!" and Mom answers, "And enough's enough." She's just joking. She said that at their silver anniversary, too.

Both Mom and Dad come from big families, so I have a ton of aunts, uncles and more cousins than "you could shake a stick at." I'm sure not all of us have the dominant vanilla gene, I mean, there must be a little hope. A little?

My two sisters and I can't help but be somewhat Vanilla, but I find you can't pray it all out. Growing up, my last name was Whitton. As I got older, I developed more of the Savage sarcasm. The Whitton humor is more like the 3 Stooges, if it exists at all. With every ounce of hope comes a bucket of heartburn.

PHOTOGENIC

I am photogenic, yet somewhat damaged. Like someone dropped a work of art. If you were looking at the real me, I am willing to bet you wouldn't believe that I wasn't always such a gorgeous sexy woman. Well, it is true.

It was the 60's. I was a big, redheaded gurgling mess. Of course, my parents didn't know how ugly I really was. They saw a fat little baby with dimples, the kind of kid you should keep feeding buttermilk and chocolate pudding until they burst. Well, they did their best. And I had 16 aunts and uncles who came over to pet the fat baby and feed it, and pinch its fat little cheeks. That's probably HOW I got dimples. And I had an older sister who brought her friends over, to see who could lift me the highest without dropping me.

So, by the time I was ready for kindergarten, I was well rounded, but not having used my legs much, they were unreliable for really difficult tasks, such as stepping onto or off of a curb. I fell everywhere I went. Now when I point to you, you say "Picture Day." Kindergarten, September, 1964. The Beatles may have been having a grand time arriving in the United States, however, I had just had a visit from my cousins Billy and Bobby. They were notorious toy destroyers. Before they came, I had about 50 dolls, none as fat as me. When Billy and Bobby decided to play in my room, my dollies suffered. No pull string was left attached, no head of hair left unburned, and no accessories ever found again. Oh, my Mrs. Beasley! Oh, Chatty Cathy! Not Barbie and Skipper!!

I cried and threatened to rat out Billy and Bobby to their parents. Then my lovely cousins chased me down and beat me up. Bobby found the scissors, and Billy held me down for my new haircut. Remember bangs? Mine looked kind of avant-garde. So I was beaten, bruised and had weird hair. I looked rather like a poster child for Kindergarten Psycho Ward. And while I was getting my new look, my cat got scared and gave me two long scratches on the right side of my face. It lent to the artistry. And, the next day was...(pointing to you now)...that's right, Picture Day.

Oh, let's move on to first grade. Still learning how to walk, I stumbled around in the backyard, trying not to bump into everything. Luckily, we had only one tree, about 10 inches in diameter all the way up. In first grade, no one had any front teeth. It's a wonder we could eat. I played a lot of Tag, because my neighbors knew I couldn't catch them. They loved to play with me. I was constantly "It." One day, after a particularly exhausting round of Tag, I ran face first into the only tree in the backyard, giving myself a concussion and a nasty purplish goose egg on my freckled forehead. There were also 2 faded cat scratches and 2 missing front teeth. If ever there was a Jo of woe, it was me. And the next day was....you got it.

The average person would come away from this whimsical childhood unscathed. But wait, there's more. Second grade. My mother had learned to make finger curls in my hair. She said I looked like Shirley Temple. The truth was I looked like a used rag mop with freckles. I got my teeth back, but they came in as giant donkey teeth, the largest known teeth of any second grader in history. Check your Brittanica. And the next day......

Do you want to re-live third grade with me? It's ok. I can take it. I had my Sunday School teacher wrapped around my little finger, and I was a very talented accordion player, ripping into the heart of "Somewhere My Love" whenever the mood struck my mother. In third grade, my teacher noticed I couldn't read the blackboard from the back of the room. What joy and what surprise to get to wear glasses for the rest of my life. So, for Show and Tell, my mother said I should take my accordion to school and play for my classmates. Yeah, that would draw them to me. Can you think of anything that would reek more of "don't play with her, she's scary" than a fat little redhead with big teeth, freckles, dimples the size of moon craters, and glasses, carrying around an accordion nearly twice her size, instantly ready to recite Bible verses? Picture day, schmicture day. I had become the definition of grace and style.

I had quite the reputation of smelly cabbage by 6th grade. Obviously, I had to push it just a little further by becoming a crossing guard (on the nerdometer, the equivalent of an adult unarmed security guard) and getting new glasses. I had never let anyone cut my bangs again, but my new glasses were diamond shaped, and my bangs sort of stuck out over the top of the diamonds like little fangs, forehead fangs. My face had sort of grown with my teeth, and now they only made little dents in my bottom lip. Then I had dimples in my cheeks AND my lip. I was becoming a woman. Any day I would be called to guest star on Mod Squad.

In Junior High, the best picture was the one right after I took a baseball bat to the teeth, playing catcher. I had black eyes, chipped and missing teeth and a bruised cheek, plus the red hair, freckles, crater dimples and fat. A kid named Harold told me I was the ugliest girl in school. I retorted, "No I'm not. Theresa Fishbaum is." He said, "Well, you're the second ugliest." My self-esteem went through the roof.

The rest of my picture days have gone by in a cat-scratched blur. Of course, I am extremely beautiful now, and quite sexy. Really. You know, I have beautiful children and grandchildren, but MY majesty is so complex that it takes a refined eye to really capture it. Let's say that Texas phrase together, "Bless her heart." I guess I HAVE been damaged in the process of growing up, but Maybelline, Avon and Playtex 18-hour girdles are doing well because of me. Not to mention Krispy Kreme.

    Unfortunately, now I'm old. When this happens, and it WILL happen to the rest of you ladies, your shoulder blades begin to look like back boobs, and the front parts of you begin to point to the floor. Yes. Oh the men still look at me intently, and they look again, but then their eyes sort of drift down. So I look down with them. Suddenly everyone is looking at the carpet, like somebody lost a contact lens. I sometimes wonder why I didn't think of this before. If I could have drawn the boys' eyes down to my toes, I know they would have liked me more. I have beautiful toes, and I can spread them out like the Vulcan greeting of Live Long and Prosper. How chic, eh? Every day I become more photogenic.

Chapter 2
VANILLA CHILDHOOD

My name is Joie. It came from Merri Jo, as an alternative nickname to JoJo. My sister named me Merri Jo. She wanted to name me Merry Christmas, since that was when I was born, but Mom said she didn't want to go around introducing me, "This is my daughter, Merry Christmas." She said they would reply, "This is my son, Happy New Year." The Jo part undoubtedly came from another Jo relative. Everybody on Mom's side of the family has a Jo and a Jack in each generation.

Unfortunately, my youth was in the era of bad sit-coms, and Petticoat Junction was pretty popular in my 'hood. So I was constantly called Betty Jo, Bobbi Jo, Billie Jo, or Uncle Joe. My mom still calls me Merri Jo, but she says it really fast and it sounds like Mare-Jo. My dad calls me middle daughter, because there are three of us, and it is really hard to remember our names. My sisters call me JoJo or Zoey.

In second grade, my classmates started calling me the girl named Joey. In sixth grade, I changed it to the French spelling, Joie, which is pronounced "jwah" but no one ever calls me jwah, well not to my face. Nowadays, I don't care if people call me any form of Jo or even Merry Christmas. I also respond well to "Oh, sainted wise woman" and "hey, funny writer lady."

My friends have trouble with the word Ma'am. It makes them feel old when the youthful cashier at McDonalds says "Would you like fries with that, ma'am?" I don't mind "Ma'am." It's respectful. You wouldn't dare to skip the yes ma'am or no ma'am when talking to my mother.

In the south there are different rules. Females under 12 are called Little Missy. From 12 to 25, you're a Miss. From 26 to 60, you're a Miss or a Ma'am. Women of retirement age are "Miz." If we make it to 90, we're "Ole Miz." Down south, if you call a woman by her first name without being related to her, them's fightin' words. Of course, the men have no such rules.

I can't remember wanting to be anything except a writer since I was very small, although my sisters tease that I have gone past the days when I could be discovered as the newest Hollywood child star. Ok, so I used to tap dance between stories. But I love to write. Storytelling is in the blood. There must be a Vanilla Journalism gene.

Being a reporter is exciting and challenging. Writers and editors are exceptionally smart people with great humor and excellent ideas. I was hooked on writing since I was three, and I wrote my first poem...

"March."
"Its March, Its March,
Birds flap and flarch."

My parents loved the poem, writing it in my baby book, and passing the sonnet along to family members, who all asked, "What the hell is flarch and why are birds doing it?" To mom and dad, it didn't matter what flarch was. They knew I had chosen a profession. And someone must have told them I could likely make up to as much as five bucks an hour in the field of journalism. They smiled happily as they realized I wouldn't have to rely on my beauty to make my fortune.

My mother's thought was that anyone who makes up words at age 3 is going to make a name for herself. She figured that if I had to dig into my imagination when my vocabulary was that small, then when it was bigger, I could make up even better words. I hate to disillusion her, but so far, flarch is my best word. It means to jump about in a birdbath.

Other words I created include: vaccicute, which is the same as vaccinate, but it hurts more; splatch, which means you made a mistake with the glue; and hork, the sound one makes when milk comes out of one's nose. Mom's dream is for me to write the great American novel incorporating flarch, vaccicute, splatch and hork. There you go, lady.

The older I get, the more blame I find I can assess to my mother. She torments me when I least expect it. For instance, whenever I hear the sound of a vacuum cleaner, I cannot function. I could be doing a relatively easy job like sitting on the couch, reading the paper, but I would go into an instant temporary coma if I heard the vacuum start up. I blame Mom.

In the 60's, cartoons were only shown on Saturday mornings from 9 to 11 a.m., on one of three channels. I would wake up anxious to watch the Roadrunner run from the Coyote, and invariably, this would be the time Mom chose to vacuum the entire house, or worse, make me do it.

We had a monster Hoover vacuum, too, the kind that could suck up dirt from the other side of the planet. It had two settings, Truck Pull and Deafen the State. I had to wait for the late 70's to hear an entire Bugs Bunny episode. For this upset, in my adult life, I am rewarded with a few moments of non-function, rather like a seizure, when anyone plugs in the Bissell. This is why I have a "conniption" when anyone drops something on my carpet.

Another thing she made me do was play the accordion. Raise your hand if you were forced to play an annoying musical instrument in your youth. You can sympathize with me, realizing that I started out with the piano, and I grumbled so much about my teacher having dog breath, Mom finally said "Ok, we'll compromise. You can quit piano, but I get to choose the next instrument." Boy did she choose. It had two settings, Annoy, and Cheese off the Entire Planet.

Apart from the sound it makes, there is another annoying accordion feature, in that short people cannot be seen over the top. When I played at a recital, people saw a forehead and curly hair sticking out of the top of this black and silver snarling and sputtering machine, with two little hands on either side and short legs sticking out below. I was the snot-nose brat making faces at the audience behind a bagpipe wanna-be. I couldn't believe it when they actually applauded. I was sick of it after the first 10 minutes, but Mom made me stick with it for 3 years, to drive the Vanilla deeper. To my dying day, I will hate polkas.

She had a dream to hear me play "Lady of Spain" while riding a unicycle, as a Miss America contestant. Not going to happen. I'm allergic to the accordion. But I love Weird Al.

My mom is also to blame for me being fat. She forced us kids to drink buttermilk. We also had to eat liver and okra, and say we loved it, because there were starving people in China. When I told her I was fat because of her making us clean our plates, she said, "Oh, yeah. My bad."

She is also to blame for my age. She could have had me 10 years later. I would have waited. She and my father also gave me my looks. It's unforgivable what some people do to their kids. She never stopped my father from trying to make me appreciate banjo music. He forced us to listen to Hee Haw and the Grand Ole Opry. Now that I'm an adult, I find that a day without country music is like a day without sunshine and a high pollen count.

In a non-vanilla world, there would be no ear assault with accordions, banjos, kazoos, bagpipes, recorders, Barney songs, Casio keyboards or vacuum cleaners. A former boss of mine told me that parents cannot take the blame or the credit for anything their children do, as we are all responsible for our own actions. I blame my mother for not teaching me that earlier.

Reading to a child shapes his personality, and turns him on to reading. I am an avid reader because before I could read, my Dad scared me with tiger tales, and he was one of the all time best storytellers.

They say to have a truly well rounded education; you should read the books your father read. Well, in my lifetime, my Dad has only read one book, "The Man-Eaters of Kumayon." You thought I was going to say the Bible, huh? Dad left the biblical education of his children to Mom. He concentrated on the stories of the great white hunter, Jim Corbett, who killed hundreds of tigers that were bent on eating residents of Bengal villages.

When he would read a story out of this book, his eyes lit up and he looked frightened by the impending doom. His voice got really thin and high when the big cats got near the children of the village and then he'd growl when they pounced and he'd grab me by the leg. It scared me to death. I loved it.

He gave me nightmares by saying things like "I bet you're glad there's no man-eaters around here," and "Those tigers must be several miles away." And there would be a look in his eye like he wasn't too sure a Bengal tiger wasn't coming down our street. My sister said, "There are NO man-eating tigers in Sparks, Nevada." I had to look out the window.

He also read stories from Outdoor Life, a magazine filled with accounts of the maimed and nearly eaten folks who had run into large hungry animals with big teeth. I began to sense a theme with my dad. He told stories of incredibly brave young men who took on angry beasts and inevitably saved babies from the jaws of death.

The children of Kumayon were inordinately unsafe. They were tasty snacks for large orange and black felines. One particularly chilling story Dad told was about a lady whose little girl (my age, of course) was fond of the rocking chair on her porch, and one day while everyone else was gone, she fell asleep in the rocker. I noted that the adults are always out working when tigers start their menacing ways.

A tiger, the biggest in Kumayon, happened to walk by, hungry of course, and looking for a crunchy brown treat. Dad said, half whispering, then louder, "The tiger woke the girl up by sniffing her hair. Before she could scream, he chomped her in half. (Dad paused while my sister and I said "Ew. Gross.") He ate her up and walked off, leaving the rocking chair in motion. (Here he makes a squeaky rocker sound.) The mother swears that when the afternoon breeze blows through the village, the chair rocks the ghost of her little girl." And then Dad paused to wipe his eyes.

Of course, none of the man-eaters survived the sharp eyes and accurate bullets of Jim Corbett. All the tigers died badly after consuming a few villagers. There was always revenge, justice and closure to a Kumayon story. But I still had dreams that Tony the Tiger ate me up and said I tasted "GRRREAT!"

Dad tells these stories about big cats so he can make the growling noise. He loves to growl and scare people. You can't take him to Kmart. Mom will say, "Bill, don't growl in the pharmacy. You scared the you know what out of that old lady." He takes it as a compliment. "You mean she thought there was a cougar behind her?" He often growls at the dinner table. Mom is used to it, but it confuses the hell out of guests who come over after Sunday school. Of course, most guests are family, and they just growl right back. But Dad is the best growler.

Growling is a learned behavior. Dad learned it by watching TV in the 60's and all those Disney movies with "nature" in them. I remember Monday nights as a child, because that was the night my older sister and I wanted to watch "I Love Lucy" but we were pre-empted because Dad wanted to watch Gunsmoke. God forbid anyone, especially Lucille Ball, to get in his way. He watched every western ever made, even the re-runs. This means that the rest of the family knows westerns inside and out, too.

Now that there are videos, Dad can watch westerns at his leisure and everyone else's displeasure. He only likes movies with mountain lions in them. He calls them "cougars" and growls, because he can. His favorite movie is "The Wilderness Family." He must watch it seven or eight times per week. Every time he watches it, he becomes engrossed in it as though it were the first time he laid eyes on it. He wonders aloud what will happen next. If someone watches it with him, he tries to make bets on what will happen next. When a bear or a cougar happen along, Dad becomes the "special effects" man. Stereophonic growling. When the little girl cries, he cries too. "Oh, she misses her mom. I miss her mom, too," he says.

Asked what he would like to do, he will walk over to the video shelf and pull out the tape of the Wilderness Family and Mom will go "Oh, God. Not that thing again." Dad just smiles and pops in the tape. Mom does a lot of gardening. But it's gardening with a vengeance. She's out there pulling weeds and muttering "Darn cougars."

I can't watch TV with Mom, either. She thinks it's my fault that people cuss on TV. She says if I'm such a great writer, I ought to write those TV people and get them to stop their evil ways. "Ever since they cancelled the Cosby Show, there's too many wretched, foul-mouthed, filthy, nasty-talkin', nekkid people on the screen and cain't nobody say nothin' nice to nobody else."

Dad agrees, saying "Buncha-junk." That's his cussword. It applies to anything he doesn't like. It used to be "Buncha-puke" but he's cleaned up his language since his grandchildren arrived.

Being the product of church-going white Anglo-Saxon Protestants who wore white gloves and shunned the evil ways of the world outside the Assembly of God, my sisters and I were not allowed to use profanity, and in fact, did not know many people who came in contact with those who would dare to cuss.

Our whole neighborhood was highly moral, even though we lived in the gambling state. In 1970, everyone on our block had two married parents and the occasional Grandma came to live with them. By 1975, all the Grandmas were gone, and so were most of the Dads. My parents stayed married to prove the statistic wrong.

As we grew up, we were told it was a sin to say real cusswords and we were severely reprimanded for even mentioning near-cusswords such as "Dang" and "gall-durned" or "absoflippinlutely."

We couldn't get a point across by saying "I swear to God." Nowadays, my daughter says "I swear to Bob." If I'd have known to whom to swear, I'd have been able to save myself from a great many bars of soap in the mouth. We'd get spankings for saying the "S" word, and its cousin, the "C" word, even though it was a word often heard in casinos. My sister Annie got smacked for saying "Crud." I received the same when I asked, "Mom, what does this mean?" and I flipped my middle finger. She slapped me and muttered, "Devil inside these children," but I don't think she answered the question.

Mentioning private body parts was also evil, but Dad broke the rules when he called peanut-butter sandwiches "peanut-sander buttwiches." That was the extent of cussing in our household until April 23, 1968. Mom, my sisters and I were in the kitchen and someone handed my little sister an egg. She dropped it and said, "Shit." Time stood still for a fraction of a minute, and I was afraid for the life of my baby sister, whom we'd only had for three short years. I knew she was a goner. Then I heard Mom laugh. Whew. It was an amazing day in history.

You always hear people saying that kids today have no respect. Maybe it is true, because we are a little more lax with the discipline than our parents used to be. I also hear, "Boy if I had acted like that when I was a kid, I wouldn't have lived to tell about it." That was definitely true for me. I had the fear of God put in me by two parents on a daily basis. I was afraid to be disrespectful or defiant; because I knew they might maim or kill. They didn't call it child abuse then; it was child rearing. And boy did they mean rearing. One of the worst episodes was when I got in trouble at church. I was sitting in the balcony during a sermon, with my hand through the rail. The front of the balcony had that textured spray stuff they used to use on ceilings and it was flaking off.

My hand found that spot and unconsciously started chipping away at the rough stuff, which began snowing on the audience below. I didn't know I was causing the snow, until the Pastor addressed me from the pulpit, asking me to stop. I was mortified.

Then I heard footsteps on the balcony stairs. My parents were coming to get me. The next service at this church would be my funeral. I began to pray 300 miles per hour "God, please don't let them kill me. I'm too young to die." Then there they were, at the entrance to the balcony. My best friend who was sitting next to me got up and moved a few seats away. Mom sat down next to me and reached for my hand. She held it tight. Dad stood at the top of the stairs, his eyes were flames. We lived three blocks away. As the closing prayer ended, I calculated my last few minutes to live.

Once home, Mom told me to go to my room and sit there. I did. I hoped their anger would wane. It didn't. In a few minutes, my mother called me to the kitchen and told me to go out in the back yard and find her a switch. I knew better than to get a thin stick. It would be better to get something more log-like, because the small ones stung for days. No logs available, I found a stick that would break easily. After the fifth swat, the stick was broken, and I survived.

It wasn't always necessary to be so violent. Mom had death-ray eyes that froze small perpetrators. She also had a mean backhand, for when we were in the back seat of the car. If a fly landed on your face when Mom was about to backhand you, that was a dead fly. She never looked where her hand was going, but she was quite accurate.

Southern women are excellent at giving threats. They anticipate the action of others and threaten accordingly and most subtly. One of the most common threats is "I wish you would..." It's all in the delivery. One must hold her mouth in a precarious yet threatening pose, narrow her eyes to mere slits, look toward the accused with certain death behind the voice, and raising the hand as if to strike, saying, "Ahh weeish yew wood trah to contradict me." This causes an immediate attitude change in the accused, or punishment follows, swift and sure.

I come from a long line of southern women more beautiful and deadly than black widow spiders. Threats were used against me when I misbehaved. I would be warned of previous children who had passed on, due to their badness. "You remember your cousin Molly Jo? She back-talked her Mama and now she's in the grave."

My mom has some phrases that could pin you to the wall. "I will whomp your grits."

"Don't make me send your behind to Jesus."

"One more whine and I will hurt more than your feelings." Later she used prayer against us. "Dear sweet Jesus, don't let me slay this child like you slayed your enemies in the Bible."

Chapter 3
MISTY WATER COLOR MEMORIES

Frankly, I remember my childhood as though it were a home movie. Do you remember those? In the 1960s, it was the popular thing for families to do together. These were 8 and 16 millimeter silent films of children running and playing and waving as they step out of the house. Just for fun, we used to play them backwards and watch people unwave and run backwards and jump out of pools completely dry.

In my case, each movie was the result of the unraveling of every special occasion or the Vanilla version of oral histories related by the elders of the village. In a surprising effort to be completely modern, my mom recently had our entire collection of home movies put to music, on two VHS tapes. She gave each of my sisters and I a copy of the two-volume set, and now we have a video history of our childhoods set to "Fly Me to the Moon."

Watching these films on tape is different than on the old projector, with the smoking bulb. You can't play shadow puppets on the wall after the film runs out, and that was half the fun. However, now we can annoy our friends with home movies. They show tapes of their weddings and childbirths, and I bring out the home movies of Vanillaville.

Volume one of the family saga is mostly a pictorial of my childhood, from the time my double-first cousin, Donnie, who is 37 days younger than me, comes to visit and we are immediately dubbed Donnie & Jo, baby royalty. We see the infants in all their toothless fat glory, Donnie with his ears sticking out like Yoda, and me looking like a miniature Buddha. Not much has changed.

We see various aunts with their '56 Chevys, and various uncles posing like Charles Atlas. We are in the front yard of my grandmother's house in Reno, where there are climbing trees, and lots of green grass. The house, trees, and Grandma are all gone now. The grass is gone too, to make way for a parking lot for a nearby casino. Progress.

My sister runs by, hamming it up for the camera. My aunt Elaine walks out in fake slow motion. What a funny gal. Funny faces, people showing off their "best side" and cool cars. The viewer is drawn in, yet repulsed by the accompanying music. The reality is scary.

Minutes later, Donnie and I have grown past toddler stage, fishing with sticks in the Truckee River and running away from our parents during the Reno Rodeo Parade of 1964. As we grew, our parents began calling us Buffy and Jody, because we sort of looked like the twins from "Family Affair." We were celebrities in our own right, due to my dimples and his allergies. The films captured all of our charm. All of it.

Then it goes into our family trips down south, with many glimpses of multi-named cousins from Mississippi and Louisiana and Texas, whom I would not recognize now. Then, there's a trip to Pikes Peak and the Royal Gorge, where I developed a fear of bridges and heights.

Next, there are new fat little babies to see, my sister and younger cousins. Now, every scene I am in is a dramatic ballet. I have learned to romance the camera. I have the soul of a dancer. My baby sister is filmed as she bravely walks down the slide in our backyard. Twirling by on the right, there I am in a frilly pink dress, just like the ballerina Barbie. Whenever we watched this particular movie, they would all say "Ahhh" when I twirled by.

There is footage of church outings, Easter egg hunts, trips, all with me in frilly dresses, my dimples continuously dimpling as I smile and dance for you, the viewer. Then there's a short spot of cousins playing in the backyard. Then a winter snowstorm in the front yard. It is winter of 66/67. I am smiling sans teeth, and throwing snow at the camera. Then its summer again, and my older sister is posing in the front yard in her cap and gown. I twirl by in a frilly pink dress.

Volume two is more trips, more cousins, and newer films of my nieces and nephews and my own children, when they were little. There's my ex-husband. I'm so glad these aren't "talkies." Some of the films were not in order when they were put on tape, because my nephews are babies, then little leaguers, then back to toddlers, then first graders.

Some time we'll take the annoying 60's music off and put the film on CD. Mom will go wild with the thought of something even more modern, although newfangled ideas are often the spawn of the devil.

One trip in particular is not on film, but is retained in the memory of all Vanillans. In 1989, we went to a family reunion in Estes Park, Colorado, one of the most beautiful places on earth. It was supposed to be a refreshing vacation. We had 16 people in a 2-van caravan from Reno to Estes Park where other relatives were waiting to play cards. No one can remember exactly who was in what van, but everyone remembers that tempers flared and tension was at an all time high, and by the time we hit Wyoming, everyone wanted a divorce, including me, and my husband wasn't even there.

Mom and Dad traveled in separate vans most of the way, but it didn't keep them from bickering. Most of the children had a walkman plugged into their ears, and the girls were apart from the boys as a bickering protection. There was no communication between vans, so you'd think there would be no bickering problems. You'd be wrong. Upon agreeing to a stopping place, one van got separated from the other, and it was one source of aggravation. My sister and I joked, "Well, we just drove by a sign that said No Livestock Allowed on Highway. Maybe they turned back." Dad was not in the mood for jokes. "You're making jest of this," he accused. He decided to be outraged for the rest of the trip.

When we finally met up, we all tried to eat at a restaurant together, which was hard because some people didn't want to sit next to other people, and they didn't want to sit next to the other, and nobody wanted to sit near Dad, and Dad didn't have his favorite spoon. Then they all fussed about who was going to pay and who was going to discipline what kid for putting God knows what utensil up his or his sister's nose, and everyone wanted to discipline everyone else, and the waitress was a target for bad, cold food, and we ended up carrying a lot of anger into Colorado.

Whenever anyone spoke to me, I said, "Don't talk to me, I'm on vacation." Everybody argued, cried, tried on their worst behavior, disciplined the wrong kid, and ignored any attempts at peace. It was the kind of situation that makes you want to spend the rest of your life in a bald-headed cult.

The next big argument came when trying to park one of the vans and the luggage container on top of the van got scraped. It was an accident, or the crime of the century, depending on who gave you the information.

When we were almost to our destination, my brother-in-law made a wrong turn, which was added to his crime of scraping the luggage container and he has yet to be forgiven. Two miles from the campsite, I discovered a strange looking Colorado bug that looked like something out of a Lewis Carroll dream, crawling along the back seat. I freaked out while my mother was driving, which made her nervously swerve, and now I was the bad guy.

Finally we arrived, and my sister and brother in law who had yet to receive criticism (although they deserved some) managed to insult my aunt. So then they became the BAD guys, and have retained the title since '89.

So we put our kids in the bunk beds and went to sleep. My daughter and my niece rolled out of their bunks and bruised their faces, requiring a trip to the emergency room, and six stitches. It was the night before the family picture day. Years later, my daughter won an award in art class for her self-portrait, painted from the photo of her bruised face. I cry every time I see it. She laughs.

The BAD guys yelled at me and my little sister for allowing our daughters to fall out of bed. It would never happen in their family, because they had discipline. My little sister said, "Yeah, well, you're also FAT." I said, "What she said." The whole week in Colorado was like some surreal movie of people walking around crying and eating.

To make your own episode of our show, all you need is some dysfunction, a variety of sick and twisted personalities, some beautiful scenery, and a choice position at a book depository window, near the family campsite on the grassy knoll. Then you, too, can enjoy a refreshing family vacation in glorious harmony.

Chapter 4
THE TELEVISION YEARS

I watched a lot of 60s TV. I was raised on it, and could tell time by it. So, I have issues. I don't like the fact that kids can watch cartoons 24 hours per day. They have the Cartoon Network, and the Disney channel, and Nickelodeon, and more channels are coming out every six months, just to keep our kids entertained. I was not afforded this luxury, even though my TV was on nonstop for a decade. There were times when we actually had to play outside, and if we wanted to play arcade games, we had to pay a quarter per game and the graphics sucked. Today, you just need to hook up a machine to your TV and you don't need quarters.

I'm angry that my daughters' Barbies had a corvette, a jeep, a jet ski, a motorcycle, and a SUV, when my Barbies drove shoes and Tonka trucks. I had to use my imagination to play. Now it isn't necessary, or even encouraged, nor is competitiveness. I find this maddening, to the point where I want to crawl into the past. So I watch TV Land. It's re-run central. I also watch old game shows in black & white, from before I was born. It comforts me.

I read that Michigan University is now offering a philosophy course based on "The Simpsons." There is also a church down south that offers morality lessons based on "The Andy Griffith Show." Well, of course this makes sense. Both offer the viewer a slice of Americana from a small town perspective.

I think the college and the church should trade lesson plans. Andy Griffith is more about how life could be, where the Simpsons is about how things really are.

College students would learn philosophic gems from Mayberry and how they should be carrying a bullet in their breast pocket rather than in their gun. Church-goers would learn that Maude Flanders goes to women's retreats "to learn how to be more judgmental." They would see how the Simpsons go to church Sunday morning and fight in the car on the way home.

I think there ought to be comparative graduate studies that mix the two shows. This would be a great subject for a doctoral thesis.

Compare Floyd the Barber and Apu the Kwiki-Mart owner. They are both successful merchants who know everyone in town and know all the gossip.

Take a long look at Barney Fife and Chief Wiggins. They each get their man, when the man is brought to them in handcuffs. But Barney was more fierce. Neither is a ladies man, but Barney thought of himself as a dashing romantic. Chief Wiggins somehow got married and had a child, but the child is the school dunce, and the wife is hardly ever on the show, like she's ashamed to be seen with them.

There were rumors in the 60s that Barney Fife was more popular than Jesus Christ. This made Don Knotts a Beatle fan.

Think about the similarities between Opie and Bart. It is a lot like the Lincoln/Kennedy comparisons. Both are rascally little boys with weird names and ugly hair. Bart is a self-proclaimed underachiever, and there were several shows about Opie getting bad grades. Later, his ambition is to become a newspaper reporter. If that isn't underachievement, what is?

Bart is mean, Opie was sweet. Bart and his teacher are enemies.

Opie's teacher became his step-mom. Both Opie's and Bart's teachers have funny last names, Crump and Crabapple. Opie had to deal with bullies while being the son of a sheriff. Bart dealt with bullies by becoming the class clown. Opie had roller skates, Bart has a skateboard. Opie called his dad "Pa" and Bart calls his dad "Homer."

Otis, Mayberry's drunk, and Moe the Bartender have a lot in common. They have issues of rejection by their families, and they love alcohol.

Ned Flanders is like Howard Sprague; both are annoying. Krusty the Clown and Otto the Bus driver compare to Cousins Goober and Gomer Pyle. In fact, Krusty and Gomer both got their own shows. Otto has one skill, as did Goober. Gomer and Goober also compare to Marge's sisters Patty and Selma. All four are beloved characters, but nobody wants to marry them.

Montgomery Burns is like the mean old store owner from Andy Griffith that wanted to evict a family at Christmastime.

Homer and Marge have been married a long time. By contrast, each season Andy Griffith had a new girlfriend until he met Helen Crump, but he never married her until the last season.

Lisa and Maggie Simpson have no definitive counterparts from Griffith's show. Lisa is, however, the sole voice of reason, which is a throwback from the 60s when all TV characters had a conscience. Maggie, who doesn't say much, but everyone loves her, compares to a little known character on Andy Griffith, a child in a cowboy hat who offered to share his peanut butter and jelly sandwiches.

Marge is like Aunt Bea. They both have blue hair and an irritating voice. They are both excellent chefs, and a little under confident. They are both co-dependent and they were both brought up to please the man of the house.

The main differences exist between Andy and Homer. You can compare the men with the times in which they lived. In the early 60s, we wanted to see a responsible, hard-working morally correct single father raising a little red-haired kid and having to deal with the inadequacies of those around him. In the age of the Simpsons, we like to laugh at a bald, bumbling, irresponsible, lazy, gluttonous father of three who can't remember the names of his children, and we watch how his inadequacies affect all of those around him.

Each show espouses the "catch phrase." The Simpsons have "Aye, Caramba!" and "Why, you little…" and "Doh!" while Andy Griffith was famous for sayings like "Nip it in the Bud," and "I reckon" and "You're a nut."

Every so often, the Simpsons throw in a musical extravaganza or a Halloween Special. Andy Griffith would sit on the porch and have sing-along with his guitar. They also had the banjo-playing Darling family from the hills.

I applaud the effort of Michigan University to get into the Simpsons heads. But I want more. I want college credit when I compare and contrast Bugs Bunny to Spongebob Squarepants. Set the world on edge by comparing old to new cartoons. Call it the Tao of Toons semester.

I also want some old mysteries cleared up. For instance, what happened to the original Darrin Stephens of Bewitched? One Thursday evening there was Dick York, and the next week there was Dick Sargent, and nobody said a thing. No explanation, just a new Dick. Did Tabitha need therapy after that?

Also, why didn't they ever mention Mike again after he got married and left My Three Sons? It used to be Mike, Robbie and Chip. Then it was Robbie, Chip and Ernie the adopted son, who was really Chip's real-life brother. Then they moved from fictional Bryant Park to real California.

There they met Katie, Robbie's wife, who had triplets, and then Steve married Barbara and adopted Dodie, which added to the mix, along with Polly, Chip's wife. But the name of the show never changed. By the time they were cancelled, they could have been called My wife, two sons, adopted son & daughter, two daughters-in-law, three grandsons and Uncle Charlie, and Mike whom we never mention.

Another TV issue rears its ugly math head. My children got to watch Square One, which helped them tremendously with their math work in school. I had no such luck. I flunked algebra. I am allergic to arithmetic.

Math has to do with logic and abstract thinking. Well, you'd think I'd be a math major. You'd be wrong. I have always had problems with math, especially story problems. They leave me with more questions and I sort of forget about the correct answer.

If a guy takes a train from Chicago to New York traveling 75 miles per hour and another guy takes a train from New York to Chicago traveling 40 miles per hour, where will the trains be when they pass each other? To me, this is not the important question. I want to know why they didn't take a plane, and why they had to go in the first place, and why the New York train is slower. And what if they saw each other as the trains passed? Would they wave? And when will I be able to visit New York?

I hated fractions, too. If Sally has two apples and 16 friends, how will she divide the apples between them? Frankly, I'd hold out for a candy bar. And who has 16 close friends? Sally must be one of those REALLY friendly girls.

Johnny has a dollar. He and his friend want candy from the store. How many Baby Ruth bars can they buy? Depends on what year it is. In my third grade math book, the answer is 10. In my daughter's math book, the answer is one and a half. I'm guessing the friend gets the half.

Half is better than none and most of the time it is better than the whole. For instance, if the glass is half empty, you can add vodka. If you have half a brain, you're about 40 percent up on the rest of us.

When you're a kid, your age is always better if you add "and a half." After you're an adult, you stop saying that. Nobody is 37 and a half.

I don't trust sales where things are half off. It just means you have to buy twice as much, and that would mean you're half crazy.

What's the difference between a half wit and a dimwit? Is a half wit just as bright or brighter? About half of us don't have the answer to that.

Another thing about half is that you have to say half ARE instead of half IS, even if half is one. Of my two kids, half of them are boys. He has half-confused me by having two children of his own, half of them girls. Thinking about math can make you half nuts.

There is a line from the Wizard of Oz where the witch tells her army, "Half of you go this way, and the other half follow me." In other words, divide and conquer. But Abraham Lincoln said, "A house divided against itself cannot stand" and he was pretty smart, so the witch lost.

In algebraic terms, we can conclude that W (witch) divided by A (army) equals F (failure) because of the D factor (Dorothy). Now Dorothy had the lion, tin man, scarecrow, terrier and Abe Lincoln on her side, so that's D to the 5th power (D5), which is greater than W and A put together.

The best math in the world was done by Abbott and Costello. Lou can prove 7 times 13 is 28. All I ever proved in math was that I was definitely allergic. When they ask a math question on Jeopardy, I start sneezing.

My biggest issue with TV these days is children's programming. I've been told my attitude is shameful, but I really, really hate...the Teletubbies. I grew up watching hours upon hours of TV, but this is one show I would seriously boycott.

I know Jerry Falwell says there are specific reasons not to idolize these characters. Well, the reason I don't like them is that they are asinine.

The premise of the Teletubbies is speaking gibberish and watching some sort of inane, painfully dull movement again and again. Woo. Kids love it. My teenage daughter loves it because I hate it.

The four tubbies look like a combination of Grimace from McDonalds and Cookie Monster with a dye job. They come in four day-glow colors, with various antennae. They have TV monitors in their stomachs, much like tacky sculpture with clocks in the stomach.

Tubby vocabulary is limited to "Uh-oh" "bye-bye" "again" and a garbled word I'm told is "Tubby custard."

When the show opens, the tubbies run over rolling green hills, giggling for about five minutes. Then one of them turns on his or her (they are androgynous) tummy TV and they all watch five or six minutes of a leaf blowing around in a gutter, or something equally brain stimulating.

Just when you think you'll explode if you watch one more second, the video clip is over, and one of the tubbies will invariably say "Again!" and they will watch the clip again, because how often does anyone get to see a leaf or a gutter? Anyone with an IQ over six and a half runs screaming from the room at this point.

My daughter tells me the tubbies have four distinct personalities and loveable traits. Oh, I guess. They certainly bring out the best in me.

She says little kids love the show because it is repetitive. I say, then why don't kids listen to their parents when THEY say things over and over again, like "Clean your room." Do parents need to dress up in some big green suit with antennae and jump around so that their kids will pick up their toys?

The end of the show is much like the beginning, with the tubbies, exhausted from watching a video, running a little slower over the hills, saying "Bye-bye."

I think this would be a much better show if (and this is where my Vanilla gene shows) there were a sniper in the hills, muttering to himself and shooting the ugly beasts. Get 'em in the cross hairs and BLAM, Oh yeah, I wish you would say "Bye Bye" now.

Don't hate me because I advocate the use of weapons on ugly, obese, brainless puppets. You know I'm right. There is nothing educationally stimulating about these characters. The words "empty" "vacant" "arid" and "banal" come to mind, along with other words not fit to print here.

I want my kid shows with some semblance of intelligent life. I don't like Barney, either, but at least he has a better vocabulary than the tubbies.

This generation doesn't have a monopoly on brainless TV shows. We had our share. When you think about it, how well did Captain Kangaroo prepare us for the outside world? We only had 3 channels, no VCRs, no computers, and a lot of children's entertainment was mindless. When they called us the peanut gallery, they referred to brain size. In general, puppets and marionettes were the first instruments used to "dumb down" American children. We were supposed to believe they were real, and cheer when Punch and Judy beat each other.

I never liked Mr. Roger's Neighborhood. I would go to the dentist to avoid watching it. I never wanted to be his neighbor, sorry. I certainly don't want to live in the rolling green hills of Teletubby land, either, unless it's legal to carry an assault rifle there.

Another TV issue is black and white. Get a big bucket of popcorn and pop in an old black & white movie and I'm there. I have a fascination with things not in Technicolor. I sometimes wish I could meet people in black & white.

When I was six, I would lie on the floor with my feet underneath the TV, my head resting on my arms, and watch all my TV shows in black & white, because color TV was for rich people. We had a 25 inch Motorola, encased in light brown Formica, on Queen Anne legs, and if anyone wanted to find me, they knew where to look.

One time, I was watching Bullwinkle and I had hooked my toes on a little ledge under the TV and pushed up. The TV came crashing down on me, smothering me with the black and white screen. It was a slow motion avalanche that knocked the air out of me. I couldn't scream. I barely gasped. Luckily, my parents were listening from the kitchen, and came running when they suddenly didn't hear the TV.

They saw me turning purple, and Dad pulled the monster off me, and Mom made sure I didn't damage the TV. She quipped, "That's not how you get on TV, missy." Really, I could have made the local news, had the TV crushed me. But it only weighed 800 pounds, and I was a tough kid, until then.

When we finally got a color TV in 1971, I missed the Motorola. I missed not knowing what color the Lennon Sisters were wearing on the Lawrence Welk show. The kids ask, "Who?" I enjoyed the mystery of black and white. Color brought everything to life when I was getting used to living in a gray world.

For my 10th birthday, my parents got me a 12 inch black and white TV for my room. It was encased in red enamel and it looked like a giant apple. They never saw me again, as I spent every waking moment in front of the tube. Mom swears it's why I wear glasses.

My favorite after-school activity was watching the "Be My Guest" show. It was the afternoon movie, hosted by one of Reno's first TV personalities. She was a beautiful blonde, on the same beauty scale as Dinah Shore or Donna Reed. She smiled and introduced the movies and made everyone feel welcome.

I loved her movies. In front of my giant 12-inch screen, I saw all the classics. I saw "Mildred Pierce," "The Sands of Iwo Jima," "Stagecoach," "White Heat," "To Kill a Mockingbird," "Psycho," and "Twelve Angry Men."

There's something about black & white that brings out the drama of a story. It nearly assaults your eyes if you see it in color. These days, I think the opposite may be true. Everyone is so used to color that black & white is left to artists like Ansel Adams, and hopefully always to "Citizen Kane."

Chapter 5
DIVERTISSEMENT

This is the continuing story of a strange dysfunctional family that still manages to hold reunions. Their motto is "We put the 'al' in 'dysfunctional'" – see? They can't even do that right. The names have been changed to protect the innocent.

Once upon a time, there was a man named Outright Ridiculous Rage. He was a bully on the playground, always starting fights, never settling down. He decided on a particular hairstyle in the early 1930s. He continues the fight for respect for the bolo tie in the world of fashion.

Rage grew up and left his birthplace, traveling west. His parents, Fitsov and Shameless, wished him well, in an angry sort of way.

On his trek, he met a woman named Hidden Sarcastic. She too had questionable taste, and a love for banjo music. They fell in love, and soon married. Now her name was Hidden Sarcastic Rage. They had a family. Three girls were born, Nita-Bein Control; Humorous Codependent; and Outta Here Soon.

Nita Bein Control was the oldest daughter and often in trouble. As a teenager, she sneaked out her bedroom window and hung around obnoxious, smelly boys called hippies. She married High

School Drop-Out, and later delivered a first class set of twin boys, Crafty and Cunning. She divorced and later remarried Whiny Terrorist. To please him, she had a second family, this time two girls named Listen and Repeat.

Outta-Here Soon was the youngest, and always in trouble in school, church and at home, prompting her permanent assignment to her bedroom until she was old enough to move out. In fact, there are no pictures of Outta-Here in the family album, because she was in her room when they were taken. For several years, only her Principal knew what she looked like.

As the middle child, Humorous Codependent was the most neurotic. She got along with everyone while secretly plotting their demise. It was lucky she never got hold of a gun, because not only would she have used it, it would probably have gone off in her back pocket. She was a super-klutz, always scratched, and burned, scraped, bruised, broken and run over. Her mother said this was just for attention. Her father agreed and said, "The next time you get hurt, young lady, I'll spank you."

Humorous Codependent, Hum for short, got straight B's and was the class clown. Always up for a dare, the only time she was in trouble at school was when she jumped off the roof of the gym. She was suspended for getting a broken ankle. As Hum grew up, she continued to fall on her sense of humor. That's how it got twisted. She became a single parent at age 17, giving birth to a son, Attention Deficit Disorder. The two of them struggled along until she met Tarnished Knight. They soon became a family and added a daughter, Artiste Withattitude. Everything was going along quite musically for Hum, for awhile.

Meanwhile, Outta-Here Soon grew up and married Man-Of-War. They had a daughter, Bright. They got divorced and Outta-Here met and married Second Marine. They had a daughter, Dramatica. That marriage didn't work out either.

Then Hum decided to join her sisters in the divorce game. Tarnished Knight remarried right away to someone who appeared to be a much, much bigger version of Hum. Attention Deficit Disorder had already grown and left home. He married Entirely Absent and they had two children, Cute and Charming. Entirely Absent then ran away, leaving Cute and Charming in the hands of Attention Deficit Disorder. Artiste Withattitude became a beautiful and multi-talented young woman, who ran away and joined the circus. There she met her future husband, Bad Dresser.

The twins, Crafty and Cunning grew up very close to each other, yet one became an artist, the other a convict. Listen and Repeat are not quite grown yet, but there is a rumor they want to change their names to Been There and Done That.

Outta Here is working on a third marriage, to a great guy named Non-Military Personnel. She has a third child, a boy named Havoc. She raises Havoc, Bright and Dramatica clear across the country from her relatives.

Hum wants no more from marriage, and seeks a permanent honeymoon status with her boyfriend, Adorable. This irritates her mother, Hidden Rage.

While they all moved away from home, there is still a lot of Outright and Hidden Rage in them all. Meanwhile, Outright and Hidden are still together in their little trailer of wedded bliss, and the next reunion has been scheduled for the hottest day of July in Texas.

Chapter 6
MIDDLE CHILD

Welcome to the middle ages. While visiting relatives at Christmas time, I came to a startling realization. Here I was, the middle of three girls, standing in the middle of the floor, between rooms, in the midst of all the people, looking for my keys.

My dreams are full of toys and death. I remember more than I forget. Some would say I'm closer to the end than the middle, but I had a late start at actual living. I forget where my keys are, but that's not the beginning of the end. I used to forget my coat on the playground. In the future, someone will probably have to remind me where I have left my teeth.

If I were spinning around three times, someone taking a picture would inevitably snap the shot on the second turn. If there's a green house with a huge green lawn and beyond the lawn an ocean of blue-green water, I would be on the edge of the grass about to step on the shore, no doubt looking for my keys.

Not very often do people even realize their beginning and middle and end times because they are busy and the times fade in and out and phase through one another. There is a little of the beginning in the middle and the end, there is a middle in the end and the beginning, and and end to the beginning, called the middle. I am the very model of the middle.

For example, during the middle, some endings are divorces, and some beginnings are new relationships, new jobs, or going back to college as a grandma. And in the middle of middle, one's child might go to middle school.

To further illustrate, I am a daughter and a mother and a grandmother. I love cartoons, yet I cannot stand noisy, disrespectful kids. I am all over the place but still in the middle.

Around my family, I am in the middle, trying not to interfere but wanting to take care of all the problems. I play with cars on the floor with my grandson while listening to CNN. I teach him my favorite joke about the middle, "Show me where the savages shot you." And he lifts up his shirt and shows me his belly button and I tickle him.

At the pool this summer, I swam from side to side right in the middle, while kids splashed in the shallow end, and adults dove from the high dive.

I can see both sides of most arguments and yet I prefer quiet to justice or controversy. However, if people are arguing, I sort of like to get into the middle of it, and slap them.

My speaker settings are at the middle; my radio station is in the middle of the dial. If someone says pick a number between one and ten, I choose five. "Midway" is my favorite war movie. I love the word "equidistant." I have central heat and air. I like peanut M & Ms, and all other candy with something in the middle, and I happen to know that Habakkuk is the 35th book of the Bible, which is just a little past the middle.

The middle letter of the alphabet is M, for middle. The middle word in Webster's Collegiate Dictionary is "nescience" which means ignorance. This may be exactly why I can't find my keys.

Not only am I a middle child, I am the generation between my father and my son. Now this is a huge gap. More like a chasm. It is a span of just 51 years, but I'm the cute chick in the middle.

My Dad has never been bar-hopping or smoked cigarettes or said a bad word in his life, so far. My son, however, had accomplished all of the above by age 15. Dad has never worn jewelry, unless you count a bolo tie. (You can't.) My son, Jack, has a pierced tongue. Dad likes banjo music, Jack likes Megadeth.

Dad wears snap shirts and polyester slacks that look like denim, from far away. Jack wears whatever shirt smells the least offensive. Neither is a fashion God.

The thing that impresses me is that with such wildly distinctive differences, they have always been the best of pals. They used to spend a lot of time together when Jack was growing up. In fact, Dad arranged for Jack's first haircut at age 2, and Jack wanted a coiffure "just like his Grandpa's" which was first discovered in the 1930s.

The gap between my grandchildren and me, 37 years, is not as well defined. I hope that as I grow extremely old, my grandchildren don't think of me as an old fogey with strange taste in music. If they do, I will remind them of Barney and Teletubbies, fuzzy purple abominations sold to their crowd.

I like my children's music most of the time. It is hard to imagine how their teenagers will shock them, like mine tried to shock me. They tried with tattoos and piercing and screaming singers in dirty flannel shirts. Big deal. Don't give me Marilyn Manson. We had Alice Cooper. Seen it.

I have entered a new yet vague boundary of earthly perdition called grandparent land. In it, everything the little children do is precious, and my own children I find tolerable, even at the adult table.

My old rules about child rearing are null and void. I have caved. I used to have a rule against toy guns. My feeling is that guns are not toys and toys are not guns. I still feel that way, and I would not buy a toy gun, even a squirt gun, for anyone.

This is not to say I didn't get tripped up by Vanilla when Jack was little. Although it killed my Dad to never get Jack a b.b.gun, Jack would pick up any other toy, even stuffed farm animals, and go around shooting them as if they were guns. It didn't go over well with me, but it made Dad laugh.

Now someone has given my beautiful little grandson a bright orange squirt gun which he aims at things while yelling "Pow!" and it is probably the cutest thing in the world. I don't understand why it is different now, but it is.

After Calvin is done "Powing" everything, he sits and "reads" a book or two. He has memorized where some of the words are, so he is obviously a genius.

My granddaughter doesn't give a rip about toys yet. She only wants to be held, fed, burped and put back to sleep. There are days when those are my goals.

I keep telling my kids I am too young for this mental change. I think of a grandmother as someone who is really old and frail, who wears funny clothes and gives out money and candy on a continual basis. I am not frail.

People continue to tell me I don't look like an old grandma. I look MUCH too young. People who really like me say I look MUCH, MUCH too young. Of course, when I was the mother of a two-year-old at age 19, I could still get in the movies for the "under 12" price. I've been asked for my identification in the gaming areas of casinos, even at age 38. This means that when I am 100, I will appear to be only in my 90s.

Mentally, though, I have become Methuselah. When I'm around my grandchildren, I suddenly walk down memory lane and every sentence out of my mouth starts with "Remember when..." And the generation gap widens.

Chapter 7
RAPTURE CHECK

It may be the end of the world as we know it. There are wars, death, destruction and really bad TV sitcoms out there. Plus, I don't know what the temperature is in hell, but it's got to be close to the temperature of metal playground equipment at the park this week. At least one kid disintegrated Saturday afternoon, leaving only a pair of toddler sandals on the slide.

I am lucky to have my Mom, because I don't make it to church regularly. Mom serves as my rapture check. If the nightly news has me worrying about the end of the world, I just call Mom and see if she's still around. If she is, I know that God hasn't raptured all the saints yet, and there's still a chance to pray my way to heaven, and kick in a little apology for missing too many sermons.

There's all kinds of bad news these days. All you hear about on CNN is war and death and anti-war protests that turn ugly. I'm lucky there's a cartoon network, because if I didn't get a break from the evening news, I'd have to own stock in Pepto Bismol. People have gone completely nuts these days – its enough to make me call my mother every day. "Still there, Ma?"

One day there was a news story featuring a festival in Georgia, in which healthy, robust young men with no shirts and debutantish southern beauties in bikinis "bob for pig's feet." It was called a "Redneck Festival" and there was a photo finish as a young man named Cephus connected with a pig foot in record time, a fat pink hoof clutched between his teeth, dripping. I was shocked, but Mom was home.

I have been shocked before. I called Mom after the release of the movie "Monkeybone." She was home. I called her when OJ tried on his glove, and when "Roseanne" was cancelled. She was home.

I know what you're thinking. Maybe Mom isn't a reliable rapture check. Well, you're wrong. She has never missed a day of church, even though one of her children was born on a Sunday. She reads her Bible and prays constantly. She can tell the difference between a Baptist and an Episcopalian at 50 paces. She is in tune with the dude upstairs – she may have inside information.

If she's ever gone when I call, I make sure to call again later. It would be good to know when the roll is called up yonder.

I used to worry about the rapture when I was a kid in Sunday school. I made myself sick thinking about where I would be when God came for all the good people. What if I was in the bathroom? Could he wait a minute? I didn't think so, because the Bible said everyone would go in the twinkling of an eye. Well, it takes me a while to get ready.

What if he came when my hair was dirty? Would he let me use my herbal shampoo before takeoff? What if I was really hungry for a cheeseburger? Where would we stop on the way to heaven? Cloud Nine Diner? I always wanted to know these things but you can't really ask a pastor because then they think they ought to put you in a "special" Sunday school class.

Because we have that fundamentalist relationship, my mother and my sisters also share some extra-sensory perception. My mother calls when she knows something is wrong. I can't tell you how many times I have burned or cut myself in the kitchen, and the next thing you know, Mom is on the phone from Texas.

My ex-husband thought it was spooky, this ESP. Well, he would know spooky. I met his parents and the first word that came to my mind was "Halloween." I had other words later.

Anyway, my family often knows what other family members are thinking or about to say. At family reunions, you hear a lot of "I knew it!" My cousin Kari and I used to say we shared a brain. But that would mean we each had half. But we write together sometimes, and turn out some very interesting work.

I hate to realize that my mother always knows when I'm broke, or sick, or pregnant. Oh, thank God we don't have to worry about that last one anymore.

The phone thing is probably the "spookiest" part. When the phone rings, I know who it is. If it's my mom or my sisters, I know what they're going to say. Ok, it's the Twilight Zone.

My older sister, Annie, doesn't even have to call. I know what's going on with her, or maybe I just don't want to talk with my brother-in-law. Sometimes we'll send each other cards that just say, "I know."

I have a really strong connection with my little sister, Jeni. Ever since we were little, we would communicate without words. We would often throw things.

When I was in a car accident and I called Jeni, she immediately knew what happened before I told her. When I got a new car, I was wondering in my head if it looked like an "old lady" car, and Jeni came up beside me and said, "No, it doesn't."

Chapter 8
VANILLA TALENT

    Because of the ever present danger of tacky clothes and banjo music, some folks may not think that Vanilla People are blessed with any talent. This is simply not true. Of course, some Vanillans keep their talent hidden. In fact, I have a talent for hiding my talent.

    Ok, I'll give you one fabulous example of my hidden talent. I can read and write shorthand. I remember this stuff from my high school days, which is the true miracle. All those circles, dots and dashes still have meaning, despite my later efforts to destroy my brain cells.

    My talented fingers once wrote my mother a letter in shorthand. My Dad thought we were conspiring against him. He thought there was some colossal joke we were about to play on him. A letter full of circles and dots made him paranoid. To appease him, I pulled out marvelous talent number two and wrote him a letter in Pig Latin. I told him not to tell Mom what it said. That made him feel better.

    My children never learned Pig Latin or shorthand, so there are two great ways to torture them. When I start to hear "Mom" too much during the day, you know, "Mom, can you do my laundry" or "Mom, can I have five bucks?" I start muttering under my breath,

"Etgay eethay ebayindhay emay, atanSay." Which is PL for "Get thee behind me, Satan."

I nearly always do my shopping list in shorthand. If you saw "/(" on your list, would you know you were out of toilet paper? This is where I have the advantage over the average shopper, and I would make a really good contestant on Supermarket Sweep.

Passing shorthand notes in church became standard practice. That way, if anybody picked up a note afterward, they couldn't be too sure we weren't paying attention to the sermon. All they could see was a bunch of squiggly lines.

I have not listed PL on my resume, nor listed it under Foreign Languages Spoken Fluently. Both shorthand and Pig Latin resemble foreign languages.

One time, my sister and I walked all over Disneyland speaking with British accents. It was so much fun. And one girl started to respond to our request for directions with a British accent. We were highly insulted, although she apologized profusely. Jeni said, "Oh, these pompous Americans!"

Another time, we visited San Francisco's Boardwalk and spoke with deep southern accents. It was not well received. It was great fun to walk along and ask folks, "Could y'all tell us where to find that ol' Gearodelly square dance place?" and watch people's eyes pop. We asked one little old lady with her poodle, "Ma'am, where d'y'all git them thar Frinch dawgs with the curly hayre?" We were going to ask her how big they get before they are slaughtered, but she walked away pretty fast.

Pig Latin has done wonders for my love life. No man can resist my silky, sultry voice asking, "Ooday ouyay indfay emay exysay?"

Most of these rare talents were explored and defined in the back seat of a white 1974 Mercury, which my mother called "Psam." The P is not silent. The name of the car was, phonetically, "puhsa'am." Mom always named her cars. Psam was short for Psamantha.

Many road trips were taken in Psam, and I believe the back seat held some special karma for development of strange talents. It could have been the result of multiple hours of watching Witchie-Poo try to steal Freddy the Flute from Jimmy, or Brady Bunch brainwashing, but my sisters and cousins and I all developed a haunting repertoire of back seat knowledge, humor and talents to keep from asking, "Are we there yet?" and risk annoying the driver.

The old shows and songs of the 60s and 70s are planted in our brains. In the area of my brain that I try to keep damp, I have a photographic memory of HR Pufnstuf, and the Banana Split Show.

If you haven't run screaming from the room yet, it is because you remember these trips. To amuse four or five pre-fourth graders, our trips would include musical interludes such as all 27 verses of "She'll be coming round the mountain" and "Found a peanut" and "There's a hole in the ground." These were followed by a plethora of good old songs from Sunday School that included spelling and shouting and they are all mixed up in my head and they come spilling out on the freeway when I'm driving, which is really frightening to my passengers.

Incidentally, the answer to "How long till we get there?" is "About an hour." You could be five minutes or five hours from your destination, but the answer remains the same.

The adults in the front seat were responsible for about half of the mental bedlam in the backseat. They would often join in the singing, or start an annoying song, just to be in control. A lot of people have trouble remembering the names of the seven dwarves, Happy, Dopey, Doc, Grumpy, Sleepy, Sneezy and Bashful, or the eight tiny reindeer, Dasher, Dancer, Prancer, Vixen, Comet, Cupid, Donner and Blitzen. Dad mixes the two groups together when he sings. "You know Dasher and Dancer and Bashful and Sneezy, Grumpy and Doris and Dopey and Sleepy, but do you recall the most famous reindeer of all? Snoopy." We love to hear Dad sing.

When he's done, someone will break into the Three Stooges Alphabet Song, which starts, "B A Bay, B E Bee, B I Bikki Bye, B O Bo, Bikki Bye Bo, B U Boo, Bikki Bye Bo Bu. The idea is to sing the consonants. It takes a group effort to have a good time. Of course,

Mom taught us the Alphabet song in two other fun ways. The first is to pronounce the sound of each letter, as in Ah, Buh, Caw, Duh, Eh, Feh, Guh,.... She also taught us to sing backwards, which is "ZYXWVUT, Stand on your head and sing with me. SRQPONM, LKJIH and G, FED and CBA, I sang the alphabet backward today."

You probably can't wait to get in a car with me, especially if you're a third grader at heart. Everyone hates the 100 Bottles of Beer on the Wall song, except third graders. They like to say beer, and they love the thought of taking one down and passing it around. This thought always made me sick, because you never knew who would backwash. I say leave the third graders at home when you travel. They are just trouble. They like cartoons like CatDog, and Spongebob Squarepants. Trouble.

If you must travel with third graders without Walkmans, I suggest an experiment in torture. Begin with John Jacob Jingleheimer Schmidt, and move on to One Banana, Two Banana, Three Banana, Four. Four bananas make a bunch and so do many more....Tra la la.

The best thing to talk about on road trips, especially if you're in the back seat, is having to go to the bathroom. This really ticks off the driver, since they told you to go the last time they stopped. I have to admit, I was the snitch. Way back then, I had the personality of a top reporter. In fact I would say, "Here's the news from the back seat....Jeni just cut one, and the rest of us would like to roll down all the windows, PLEASE." If you start talking about toilet habits, inevitably, someone will have to go soon. It is hysterically funny to a back-seater to cause an urge in an adult. It was almost as good as making milk come out of someone's nose.

One trip to Arizona was frought with toilet humor. There was an ad for a drug store selling cologne. It said, "Best toilet water in town." We got the biggest kick out of that in the back seat. We made up our own testimonials. "I tried the toilet water across the street, and it stunk up the room."

"My dog loves Gordon's toilet water, and so do I." Next, there was a sign reporting where you could rent port-a-potties. Like people are driving down the road wondering, "Darn, I wish I knew where I could rent a toilet." And then, BAM. There they are, saved the suspense.

Driving through Las Vegas with my cousins Donnie and Greg in the car, we saw a sign for a motel with a heated pool, but the "L" was missing from the pool. So Donnie held his hand out to the rest of us, and offered the motel's finest heated poo. He had a crazed look in his eye and when he said the word "poo" his voice went up a couple octaves. It slayed us. We all cracked up, prompting the admonition of several adults not to giggle or speak. But a few miles down the road, Donnie looked at us and held his hand out, as if offering the best of the motel. We all cracked up again, prompting the adults to change drivers due to stress. In another few miles, Donnie did it again, and again. It is 30 years later and I bet he could still get a laugh.

Chapter 9
VANILLA POETRY

Since I wrote about March and flarch, I have written a few more poems, however, none quite as observant. Well, maybe. When my daughter was a senior in high school, I went through the worst financial crisis so far. Broke was my middle name. So I wrote a theme song, and stole the tune from "My Favorite Things" from the Sound of Music, however, the lyrics are mine.

Feel free to sing along.
These Are A Few of the Bills I Must Pay
"Yearbooks, ID cards and new clothes for P.E.,
Prom gowns and school clothes and shoes that are pretty;
Lab fees and club dues and new school supplies;
These are the things that make blood pressure rise...
Portraits for seniors and embossed announcements;
Class rings and field trips regarding commencement;
Gold mortarboards and accompanying gowns;
These are a few of the bank trips to town...
(Bridge) When the rent's due, and the cable, and the power, too;
There's a new thing for seniors to purchase right now,
And that's when I feel so blue...

Next year is coming, with college tuition;
This year's bright seniors have lots of ambition;
Full four-year scholarships might pave the way;
But I need Mighty Mouse to save the day...
Someone should warn us that costs are enormous;
And funds are all due now, they've just informed us;
We never dreamed when our kids were just five;
That 13 years later no money would survive...
Why is it most things cost three hundred dollars?;
When did the prices make you start to holler?;
How is it possible "they" know how much;
Money you make and that you'll never touch....
(Another bridge) I need money, lots of money, just to pay the bills;
And then I remember the wage that I make, and trust me there are no thrills.
It makes me mad to spend all kinds of money;
When I don't have any, it's just not funny;
But for my daughter, I take on more debt;
Somehow we'll get by – don't give up just yet...
I'm not so poor that I have to eat cat food;
But at the same time, I'm not in the best mood;
When people say that they need all my cash;
It's for the kid so don't bat an eyelash....
(Yet another bridge)
When we see them, with diplomas, walk across the stage;
We'll simply remember how precious they are, and be glad we're not their age."

Ok, it is a long song. I was broke a long time. I was tempted to take my new song to the street corner and pass a hat for donations, but I'd probably end up in jail for disturbing the peace. I don't sound too much like Julie Andrews. But I figure if that guy Baz Luhrman could make a song about sunscreen to fund his kid's senior year, I ought to be able to rip off Rodgers and Hammerstein for mine.

Chapter 10
FAMOUS VANILLANS

David Bowie first sang about it when I was in high school, and later, it was a TV show with a lot of dancing and singing, but we all knew about fame much earlier. My family is used to show business delight, often being asked to perform at church functions. We were big fish in a baby pool.

My sisters have awesome singing voices, and I am comic relief. In addition, Mom plays the piano and Dad plays the violin, only he calls it a fiddle. He can also play the saw. I thought up skits and played tribute to a Lily Tomlin character, Edith Ann. I wrote her a Christmas story skit that slayed the Christian ladies for years, although I think some of the ladies thought I was just retarded.

My mother often performed at church lady functions in her alter ego she called "Miss Fortune." This was a mixed up character along the lines of Amelia Bedelia.

One year we put on a funny fashion show for Mothers Day. The church ladies gathered for tea and luncheon, and we gave them Hollywood. We had a lady wearing a cardboard cut-out of a house, her housedress. One lady brought her dog and attached it to her dress with a sling made for broken arms, it was her poodle skirt. Another lady had cotton balls all over her dress, a cotton dress. My mother wore a Chiffon dress, made out of; you guessed it, toilet paper. I wore two sweetheart straws, for an elegant straw hat. My daughter wore a ten gallon hat, made by stringing together 10 empty milk jugs.

I have a truly famous cousin, Greg Proops, the comedian. Yes, even Greg has a tinge of Vanilla. His mother is my mother's sister and they have Mississippi in their blood. The whole family is star struck over Greg. We're so proud of him.

My brother-in-law, Paul took my sister Annie to Hollywood to be on "The Price Is Right" with Bob Barker. As if that weren't Vanilla enough, they wore matching shirts (Paul and Annie, not Annie and Bob Barker) and they sat in the back, waiting for the announcer to say "Come on down!" Then it happened. Paul got called down, outbid an old lady by a dollar, and won a bar with barstools. They don't drink. Then, he played the game where you guess the numbers in the price of a new car. He did it. He won a Geo Prism. Now he really thinks he's something.

At Thanksgiving, we had to endure the story of "How I Won A Car" about 437 times and how he talked to Bob Barker and the spokesmodels, bleh, bleh, bleh...And we had to watch the tape of him winning. He had his brush with fame, and he didn't realize we were already familiar with the concept, being sought-after performers with the Assembly of God. But then again, none of us, including Greg, ever won a car on The Price Is Right.

Everyone I know has had a brush with greatness. Not so much me, but everyone else. Well, Judge Mills Lane once spoke to my high school government class. My sister Annie not only met Bob Barker, but years ago, she spoke with Dennis Weaver. He was sleeping on a poolside lounge at a hotel, and she went up and asked for an autograph. He told her to go away. Now she can't stand re-runs of Gunsmoke.

My little sister, Jeni, extended her fame beyond church. No one who worked at John Ascuaga's Nugget in Sparks, Nevada in January, 1978 will ever forget her 13th birthday. It was a typical birthday celebration, to be sure, with our family eating dinner in the Pancake Parlor.

After dinner, we would sit and talk while the staff prepared a birthday cake with a great big sparkler on top. Then the waitress would bring out the cake, and everyone in the restaurant would sing "Happy Birthday." That was the plan. That's not how it worked out.

The waitress had just lit the sparkler and was headed toward the table, smiling proudly. Jeni was smiling. The family was smiling. Suddenly, from out of nowhere, it seemed, another waitress came barreling into the room backwards, pulling a cart of dishes. The cake waitress had no idea someone was backing up so close by. The waitress with the cart had no idea there was a lit cake so close by. They collided like a slow motion car accident. The sound of the crash was like brakes squealing and someone getting their breath knocked out of them, like a whoop.

Everyone's eyes were glued to the scene. There was no noise as our waitress lost control of the birthday cake and it shot out of her hands like a driver's side airbag. Jeni watched the path of the flying cake as it hurtled through the air at an enormous speed like a meteorite burning up in the earth's atmosphere. It splattered across the room on the carpet, about six feet from our table. The carpet was slightly burned by the sparkler.

The waitresses caught their breath, ours had tears welling up. The silence continued for about a minute, and then Jeni laughed this hysterical loon laugh. A combination ha ha hoo hoo hee hee haw. She couldn't stop. And it was contagious. The whole restaurant was practically in tears from the belly laugh started by my sister.

Every patron cheered as a new cake and sparkler came out after the mess was cleared. It was an awesome birthday, and our cake waitress, Aggie, never forgot to tell other "birthday" patrons about the famous flying cake incident.

Other family members have met really famous people. I'm jealous. My boyfriend once met George Peppard. My Uncle Don was once seated next to Mae West on an airplane. My Uncle Steve met Jimmy Durante twice, once at age 35, and again at age 50. Durante remembered him, too. My friend once got to meet Donny Osmond. That was torture for me. Another friend met Vic Tayback. Another met Wynona Judd. I even know someone who once met the Governor of Iowa. One of my old bosses told me he was an extra on location during the filming of Jaws, and got to be a "running away from the shark" guy and eat cafeteria food with the stars. "WOW!" I said. "When I go to Disneyland, I might get to meet Mickey Mouse."

Chapter 11
IN-LAWS OUTLAWED

Someday, some of us are going to go to heaven, and when we get there, no relatives, government employees or customer service representatives from long distance companies are going to mess it up.

I'm thinking there won't be any of the normal, ordinary awful stuff we have to deal with every day, like the DMV or a PG&E bill; otherwise they wouldn't call it heaven. I doubt if there will even be phones. Communication is likely to be telepathic.

The Bible says there won't be any marriage in heaven because that would preclude any "in-laws." These are people we can do without.

My brother-in-law, Paul, for instance, is on the "Must be slapped" list, due to his chattiness. He called on a weekend at 5:40 a.m., to discuss my children and what I need to do to help them. I don't remember thinking how much I appreciated his effort to communicate. That thought did not seem to cross my mind. In fact, what I was thinking was "God please punish those who call me before 6." I knew better than to pick up the phone, with what was running through my mind, so I let my machine answer and I drifted back to sleep, dreaming of guillotines and chopping blocks and large one-eyed men with axes.

When I returned the call much later, he answered in his cheery little voice and I asked, "Is someone dead?" He said no. I said, "Don't ever call me before 6 a.m. unless someone is dead, and it ought to be someone I like." I'll send him a list.

Other information I can do without in early morning hours is parenting advice, especially from my brother-in-law. The rule is simple. If I haven't had coffee yet, don't criticize me.

Regarding parenting, I have learned that we are simply the tour guides at the museum of life, keeping the kids behind the rope and hoping they don't spill their Big Gulps on priceless artifacts or wake up the mummies. Those would be my kids climbing on the dinosaur bones.

I try to hold my tongue when people gossip about bad parents. I criticized my own mother and she said it would come back to haunt me when I had kids. Hmm.

She told me when I was 15 that I couldn't see Alice Cooper in concert because he wasn't the sort of person I'd see in heaven. I told her she was prejudiced against a rock and roll legend. She replied that she wasn't sure Elvis would be there either.

I sometimes can't wait to get there, just to see who shows up. My kids will make it, but they'll be playing Frisbee with their halos. My brother in law will be hanging out at the Gate, with his own list. Mom and Dad will have a mansion with a front porch. Mom will communicate with me telepathically, "Seen Alice Cooper yet?" I think I'll move to an outlying cloud.

Chapter 12
FOOD FIXATION

It's food season. After Halloween, everyone gets out their big red cookbook and starts thinking of feast food for Thanksgiving and Christmas and the holiday parties in between. I am lucky enough to have six people in my family with birthdays in November and December. They also want a feast in honor of their births.

I worry about buying enough food in case I really blow it, and then I will have enough left over to try again. What usually happens is it comes out ok, and I have all this stuff left over, but it's ok, because there is another feast the next week. But I can't make the same thing I did last week, so I go buy a ton more stuff and it turns out ok and then I have a lot more stuff left over.

The day of the feast, don't even talk to me. I want coffee, I want peace, I want no children in sight. I want all men out of the kitchen. If someone does talk to me, they must maintain low tones and say how wonderful I am. Don't talk about how the dinner will turn out, you'll jinx it.

I have ruined three holiday dinners due to extreme circumstances. On Christmas, 1977, I had just had a baby, and was incoherent and I left the stuff you're supposed to take out of the turkey inside. I also burned the dressing, undercooked the sweet potatoes and the gravy was lumpy. Nobody said a word; they just fussed and cooed about the baby, which led to my new rule. "Never cook after childbirth."

The next rule came in 1988, when I had major dental surgery just before Christmas. Not only was I loopy, I put way too much salt in everything and I found a lot of food in my plants afterward.

In 1996, I learned to check the size of the turkey against the size of the oven. Unfortunately, I did not learn this before cooking the turkey.

Chapter 13
FAMOUS FOR OUR ROCKS

All of a sudden, one of my remote cousins has made the paper in Wyoming. He couldn't help it. As you may be aware, my family's motto is "React to all situations in the most illogical way."

It seems a grizzly bear picked a fight with my kin named Ken and he punched the bear in the mouth.

According to the Jackson Hole News, my Dad's cousin, Ken Bates (He actually spells his name Knn, due to his Sioux heritage, but I always knew him as Ken.) was fishing in the Snake River on Easter Sunday morning and turned around to see a 600-lb grizzly bear standing behind him. The article quotes Cousin Ken, "He (the grizzly) seemed upset about something." Members of my family are clearly perceptive about animal disgruntlement.

Given the knowledge that a disturbed grizzly was behind them, a logical, clear-minded person would react in a reasonably normal way, retreating as fast as possible, getting the heck out of Dodge. Right? Or they would be doing what the bear experts advise – play dead when encountering a grizzly. They call this common sense.

Well, to my cousin, a bear with issues and attitude problems was obviously in need of a punch in the nose. Yep. Rather than avoid serious conflict, my cousin waited until the bear lunged and grabbed, then he spun around and hit the bear in the mouth. He told reporters, "I was trying to hit him in the nose. I hit him with everything I had. He let go and kind of set back on his rump. I didn't think I could knock a bear down."

Not waiting for a 10-count, Ken pulled out one of the rocks he had in his pocket and beaned the bear on its head. A second rock hit the retreating bear on the rump.

As a tradeoff for scoring the knock-down, Ken broke his knuckles and his arm, and has to endure rabies shots. Meanwhile, the bear is looking for other fishermen along the Snake River.

I learned a few things from this encounter. For one, Easter Sunday is always noteworthy in my family. Secondly, I learned more than one of my relatives carries rocks in their pockets, as a survival tool.

One time, my Dad showed off his macho attitude in a Volkswagen. My Uncle Don was driving, and there were three kids in the back seat. We had just gone to Dairy Queen to get ice cream, and Dad was holding it in his lap bringing it home. The car hit a bump and ice cream splattered my Dad. His immediate and bizarre reaction, rather than risk laughter, was to whip out a huge hunting knife and scrape ice cream off his pants, with an extremely angry look on his face. He didn't cut himself or his slacks, but nobody dared laugh, or ask for a banana split.

There was no air in the car because when we all saw the knife, we each took a deep breath and held it for two blocks. When we arrived at the house, Don asked, "Got those pants clean yet, Bill?" Dad smiled, re-sheathed the knife, went into the house and didn't talk to anyone the rest of the day.

Even the next generation is infected. At the tender age of two and a half, my daughter saw her 18-month old cousin crying. She walked up to the crying baby, presumably to comfort her. No. She slapped the toddler on the side of her head and said "I don't wike your attitude."

No one in my family had much sympathy for criers and whiners. I biffed it really good once right in front of the house, trying to ride my bike with no hands, falling and bumping my face on the sidewalk. It was a classic case of "Look Mom, no hands!" "Look Mom, no teeth." I recall my loving mother's reaction. She was sitting on the porch howling, holding her sides from laughing. I suppose it's good she didn't have any rocks in her pocket.

We all know that deep abiding love is the glue that holds families together. And in my case, a good sense of humor and a large supply of Band-Aids was vital.

Family members have been teasing Ken, whose new nickname is Punchy. My Dad told him, "Y'all better watch out. One o' these days you'll run into a bear that'll punch back." This is the kind of advice only heard in my family.

Chapter 14
VANILLA JUDGEMENT

Who would have believed judgment day would come so soon? I'm about to get it. I don't know if you've ever been a bit intimidated by the appearance of powerful southerners, but it is sort of a Pepto Bismol moment. It could be because I'm about to be judged on my vacuuming, but I'm a little uneasy.

My aunts and my mother will be in town next week. I have not yet begun to dust. There are several names for this event, but I hear they are calling it a "visit." The last time my mother told me about a visitor coming to see me, monthly, it was unpleasant.

I'm a little nervous. I love my aunties. I haven't seen them since Ma & Pa's 50th anniversary, and before that, it was quite a few years.

Aunt Doris is the mother of my famous cousin, Greg. She is an awesome lady. She cooks up a 12-course meal in under 10 minutes, and everything always turns out fabulous, better than Martha Stewart. She has been everywhere and done everything, and she now chooses to live in a trailer in Texas. Go figure.

Aunt Marj is the family Democrat. They take her along on trips because they like to argue with her and make her ride in the back seat. She lives in Arizona and I always thought she was rich because she was the first person I ever knew who had her own milkshake machine.

Aunt Nita is the sexy aunt, getting the wolf whistles even at age 78. Her name is Juanita Frances and she leads a double life. Some of her other relatives call her Frankie. I always knew her as Nita. She lives in Oklahoma now, so we all speak a little slower around her.

Mom is the troublemaker when she's with my aunts. (We call them aints because of the Mississippi in us.) The group got together in Texas and are out "visiting" over the countryside. There ought to be a public warning.

When they come to visit me, the first thing we'll do is go out to eat. Then they'll tell my daughter the oral history of the Savage clan, reciting who begat whom and how many cousins named Charlie Joe we have.

Then we'll go to a store and Mom will try to argue with the cashier about prices. "That ain't what its wuth. Tell you what. I'm willin to give y'all two dollahs." It could be a top of the line TV or VCR, or a Rolex or even a Cadillac. Mom maintains there ain't much stuff worth more than two dollars. She would argue with a bar code.

The fab four, as I call them, have shaped my personality. Well, a little. I can't blame them entirely. What we all have in common is the art of wearing silly hats. See, you have to reach for those hidden talents.

Actually, they all represent the strength of the southern belle, and they believe that we are all souls with bodies, not bodies with souls. None of them would ever stifle an opinion. My mother in particular would be happy to "tell you the truth" about anything. Yeah, that's where I got it.

To get along with mom and the aints, you have to do what they tell you and like it. There is a southern word, "Y'otta." It is short for "you ought to." and is usually followed by "be grateful for that. I nevuh had it s'good when I'z a yungun." These ladies are masters of having had it worse than me.

To hear it told, their childhoods were filled with picking cotton and eating dirt, walking 50 miles to school and back every day, uphill, both ways, barefoot, over shards of glass, carrying their brothers and sisters through the snow. This was when they were allowed to go to school. Most days they had to work in the coal mines in the morning and the cotton field in the afternoon and the sweat shop in the evening, and they were never paid more than a few pennies each year. When they got home even one minute late from the sweat shop, their parents and neighbors would take turns beating them nearly to death. Then, they'd get about 20 minutes of sleep on a hard bed which they shared with 10 or 12 siblings and livestock. Then they'd start over the next day, and they appreciated every single minute of their lives, not like us ungrateful children of today.

I am still in the "children of today" category, even though I am a grandmother. Its not big time denial, it's just that the fab four are ageless and immortal. They simply think of most of their relatives as "children." It cain't be helped.

You watch. When my California friends say I have a Texas accent, the fab four will say I ought to be grateful, because my ancestors never had an accent when they were young. They couldn't afford it. I must be lucky.

One thing the fab four do when they get together is play rummy. Generally, old ladies playing cards is not a party everyone would want to crash. However, the fab four make it extremely entertaining. As they hold their cards, they go over the rules of the game at the beginning of each hand. Then they accuse each other of cheating. Then one of them wins the hand and proves to the rest that she WAS cheating. Then they forget what the rules are again, and they make up some new ones.They love when new people join the game. This way, they can gossip and spout out such amazing bits of southern wisdom that you will just cry.

During a particularly long card game, I told my Aunt Nita that someday, I might get married again. She blurted out, "Oh that's good. Just make sure you are sexually compatible." I started to choke on my food.

My 89 year old Aunt Doris said, "Oh, you don't have to have sex. Just pinch his tushie. That's what I do." Aunt Nita said, "Well, don't get married without trying the merchandise. You could get a lemon, like my last one." My Aunt Marj said, "Oh, good night. Stop talking about sex and just play your eight of spades."

My mother had begun praying aloud. Aunt Marj told her to pray she gets the card she needs. Mom said "I am prayin for all y'all, especially you." She was looking at me. "Don't go pinchin' any tushies. God'll getcha for that." Then she looked out the window, as though certain of impending lightning strikes.

Aunt Doris mused, "You know, some tushies are straight from God." Aunt Marj replied, "Amen. Now play your eight."

Yeah, if you want to enjoy your Friday night, I recommend a card game/sex talk/prayer meeting with a group of four fabulously Savage women.

Chapter 15
VANILLA PAST TENSE

Did you ever notice how certain things you see in the grocery store can trigger certain childhood memories? You'll see a common household product, and you'll get a picture of your past in your head. That is why you'll see people standing in the frozen food aisle, with a far away look in their eyes and a big grin.

They're not mentally ill. They're remembering the good old days when they used to lay down in the frozen food and play funeral parlor.

I can go up to my little sister and say "black cherry soda" and she will start cracking up and snorting. She's not a candidate for a rubber room. She's remembering a time more than 20 years ago, when we lost any sense of decorum two Vanilla girls ever had. See, life is a bunch of Kodak moments that happen when you don't have a camera. You have to remember it with head pictures and trigger phrases.

Our black cherry soda moment came when Jeni and I took a road trip to Arizona, with my two-year-old son, Jack. He was completely afflicted with the terrible twos during waking hours. In the desert, I got stopped by a cop, and Jack asked him, rather enthusiastically,

"Are you hauling her to jail?" When I simply received a ticket, Jack was very impressed. From then on, when he misbehaved, he asked if I was going to give him a ticket. I thought this was ingenious. I knew I was going through a lot of scratch paper when Jack presumed he was in trouble and said, "Uh oh, ticket time."

On the way back from Arizona, I had been driving in the hot sun and we were all rather irritable. It was the kind of irritable you get before the sun bakes your brain and you end up in an institution. We needed relief. We didn't get much, with Jack whining in the backseat. He kept asking if we were on the right road, like he knew we were lost. We were, but we didn't want to hear it from him.

We were delirious and telling knock knock jokes and laughing like crazy even though nothing was too funny. Finally, we stopped at a tiny store to gather our senses and get a cold soda. We got back on the right road, and Jeni had just opened her black cherry soda when I said, "Knock Knock." She said, "Who who who is there, heh heh heh" and I said "Sam and Janet."

"Sam and Janet who ha ha ha?" "Sam and Janet Evening,..." I sang. And Jeni spewed forth all her black cherry soda. It was all over her, me, my dashboard and window. It was like the old Abbott & Costello skits where Lou gets spit on.

From the back seat, a little voice said, "Uh oh. Ticket time, Aunt Jeni." And we lost it again. I couldn't stop laughing. I had to pull over. We must have been a sight, two dripping women and a bewildered baby, laughing and bending over, holding our sides, trying to clean up the inside of my Toyota.

Another memory from that road trip happens every time I am in the produce section of the grocery store. When I took Jack to the store in Arizona, he saw a watermelon for the first time. He said, "Oooohhh! BIG Pickle!" and he cracked up everybody at Food King.

Family members still offer Jack watermelon and say, "Want some big pickle?" and he chuckles like they wrote it. He says, "I've known the difference for awhile, now." They don't care. They just see a fat little baby pointing at the watermelon, amazed at the size of Arizona pickles.

Chapter 16
VANILLA NIGHTMARES

One time I played a joke on my son and his friends while they were watching a horror movie. He had a plastic rat, because I wouldn't let him have a real one, and when no one was looking, I poured a few drops of Kool-Aid into the mouth of the plastic rat. Then I carefully placed it near the boys and when the red Kool-Aid trickled out, I said, "Oh my God, that rat is bleeding!" and Jack and his tough little 14 year old pals jumped and screamed. That was fun. Don't worry. He wasn't affected much.

I can't help it. I love scary stuff, probably since the Tiger stories. I adored Night Gallery and the Twilight Zone and the Alfred Hitchcock show and Outer Limits. I love Godzilla. I am enamored with Stephen King and Dean Koontz. I love the X-files and all that junk about ghosts, witches, other realms, psychotic serial killers, cannibals and bleeding rats. Halloween rules.

You're wondering if all that stuff caused me to have nightmares. Yes, it most certainly did. Ever since I first saw giant tarantulas crawling across my 12-inch black & white screen, I have had monsters interrupt my REM sleep.

In my dreams, I can outrun a hungry T-Rex, a giant furry

monster, a crazy killer clown, an alien, a wolf-man, a tarantula, and Kathy Lee Gifford. I dreamed she was a 90 –foot carol singer. It was frightening. So, my PF Flyers hit the pavement, and I zoomed off.

The monsters chase me all night, and I run forever. In waking hours, I couldn't run half a block without passing out, cussing. But I run and run in dreams, and every time I look back, the monster is about 20 feet behind me, smiling with big teeth.

It used to be bad for my parents. They heard me screaming several times as T-Rex got closer and closer. Then my mother and I discussed medication. We also talked about the differences between dreams and movies and reality, and she pointed out that movies and TV shows had commercials. So, I learned to put public service announcements in my dreams to remind me they were dreams.

Now when I get really scared in a dream, I will see an image of a TV and a voice sort of like Phil Hartman's will announce, "This dream is being brought to you by your twisted brain. The images you see are nowhere close. Chill out."

It works pretty well. I don't scream. Now I wake up, and I have to read a book to get back to sleep, and usually I have King or Koontz close by, so I start the entire process again.

Almost every time I dream, it picks on my conscious life. I will be dreaming I'm at a party and some Antonio Banderas type is talking to me, and he says, "Let me play this romantic CD and dance with you." So he puts the CD in the player, and it sounds just like my alarm clock, and it takes me a moment to realize it isn't just a bad CD, and I actually have to leave the party. Bummer.

Or I'll dream I'm back in third grade, walking to school and the teacher told me I'd lose a recess if I was late again. So I'm crossing the street and the tardy bell rings and it sounds just like my alarm clock, and I'm so grateful not to be in third grade again that I am glad to wake up.

Another dream scares me now, though I dreamed it more than 30 years ago. I was walking around the house late at night.

Everyone was asleep. I opened the back door and there was a lady with long black hair out in our back yard, wearing a white gown. She pointed toward the house with no expression, and I heard clomping footsteps behind me. I turned and went into our kitchen, where there was an enormous angry moose with big red eyes. I can still see it in my head, and it is still scary. I screamed until my Dad came into the room and walked with me into the kitchen to check and see if there was a moose. The really strange part is that my little sister had the same dream, five years later.

We concluded that the spirit of an angry moose lived in our mother's kitchen, although it was another species not indigenous to Nevada. We thought maybe there was some kind of moose burial ground under the stove. Hey, nobody knows where Bullwinkle's ancestors rest. They could very well be under a kitchen stove in Sparks, Nevada. Deep underground. Angry.

They say having nightmares is an indication of discord in your life. Nah, I think too much vanilla.

Chapter 17
VANILLA, THE NEXT GENERATION

Sadly, I must report my children are pierced. I have seen a lot of pierced people, lately. It's a strange metallic world, anymore. Everyone and their Grandma have pierced ears. An inevitable response to years of dulled senses reacting to jewelry advertising. It has become rather benign.

What is not so benign is this rush toward creating holes in parts of the body where no hole had gone before. First of all, OW! Stabbing metal through skin hurts. Secondly, who decided it would be pretty to have sterling silver skulls and crossbones hanging from one's chin? Why do we need our birthstones protruding from our noses or gold rings through our eyebrows, pointing ever westward?

One hole per ear is not enough anymore. Now one must have earrings completely ringing each ear, even up in the cartilage less than a centimeter from the skull, so that one can wear all his earrings at once. Have these people not heard of a jewelry box?

Look at the eyebrow ring. Doesn't it look like they completely missed the ear? One time my son got stitches over his eyebrow due to a skating accident, and I was in the same room when they were sewing him up and they were moving his face over his facial bones and the room got really warm and blurry and I fainted. Three years later, he got the same eyebrow pierced. He expected me to faint again, I suppose, but I surprised him. I said, "You turned your head at just the wrong moment, didn't you?"

So he got his tongue pierced. When will they learn they can't shock me? I said, "So now you can never eat hot soup again. How smart is that?" "Ith not that bad," he said, "geth over ith." Some of his friends had their noses pierced. Now they whistle when they laugh. I wonder what they'd do if they had bad allergies like mine. I could never pierce my nose. I'd be sneeze-impaired. One girl told me it felt like getting hit in the face with a basketball to get your nose pierced. "But it felt fine about an hour later." Oh, sign me up. I don't know whether they're trying to prove they have nerve or dull nerve endings.

Pierced belly buttons are in. If you look at one close up, it looks like it hurts. I watched my daughter change her belly button ring once and I had to run to the next room. Ick. Another practical reason not to get a needle through your stomach; belly button rings are more expensive than earrings and you only get one. Plus, it could get caught on your zipper, depending on whether you wear your pants properly. Kids don't worry about that. They let the pants slide. The pants slide so much, it reminds parents of when the kids were toddlers, and they had a reason for droopy drawers.

Okay, let's get tattoos, you say. Uh unh. I don't understand why this generation loves pain. Carlin said people used to get tattoos because they wanted to be one of the few people who got tattoos and now we get tattoos because we don't want to be one of the few people without a tattoo. A tattoo involves needles and ink injection into your skin (ew!) and you have to live with whatever you decide is so cute, until the day you die or have laser surgery to remove it. What fun.

I love to hear Groucho Marx sing about Lydia the Tattooed Lady, but for decoration, I think I'd rather buy a temporary rose bud than live with the Wreck of the Hesperus on my behind forever. How cool is that anaconda with fangs going to be when you're 75 and it looks more like a worm with a hat? People never think of wrinkles, but they lurk in our future.

It is sad, and I have begun the journey south, myself, but eventually, even the cutest cheerleaders begin to SAG. It is hard to be fierce when your arms jiggle. A distorted tattoo won't help at that point.

My idol, Cyndi Lauper, got a tattoo of a dragon around her ankle, where it really hurts to get stabbed with a needle, and she told David Letterman, "I couldn't walk for a week...Isn't it pretty?" Gosh, I hope it stays pretty. I hope when she's 90 she doesn't look like she has ringworm.

My cousin Kari has "Savage" tattooed across her breast. I think its an awesome play on words, you know, the Savage breast, but I keep thinking about old age and lurking wrinkles and other distortions of time, and I worry. Kari is gorgeous, but when she's 90, will the S be under her arm? Avage? And will 90-year-old breasts ever be considered Savage, outside of National Geographic?

And what happened to poor old Lydia? "She once knocked an admiral off of his feet; the ships on her hips made his heart skip a beat." When her skin headed south, I bet those ships sank. She ought to get her ears pierced.

JACK

My son Jack recently turned 24. Since I was very young, 5, when I had him, we sort of had to figure things out as we went along. I had a difficult time.

My mother's curse proved true. Since I had trouble keeping my room clean, and I had my share of sarcasm and I dared to question authority, I "had a kid who acted worse than I did." And my mom laughs.

Always clever, expressive and full of fascinating ideas and

disgusting noises, when Jack was 18 months old, he began the "terrible twos." I hope it's over soon. When he turned into a teenager, I turned to heroin. Not really, but it has been a trip out of this world.

He had a strange, sort of twisted sense of humor, even as a young baby. I don't know where he got it. He would sing Rock-A-Bye Baby and when he got to the part where "down will come baby, cradle and all," he'd say, "Boom, Dead" and laugh his head off.

When I taught him that everyone and every thing had feelings, he picked up a rock and dropped it, and said, "Oh, it fell on its head."

To call him an animal lover would be inconclusive. He is fascinated with all living creatures. He has always picked up and brought home all manner of bugs, slugs, reptiles, fish and rodents and other strays and wanted to keep them. I did not share his enthusiasm.

I complained from the beginning that he didn't come with an instruction booklet. Mom said, "The Bible, that's your handbook." I said, "Mom, there's nothing in there about what to do when he tries for a world's record burp in Sunday school." Or when he picks apart clocks and radios and can openers and the infinite number of parts and a significant amount of glue are scattered over his floor. Or when you find lizards in the laundry, or when all the forks are in the backyard for a scientific experiment. For the handbook to have worked there would have to be an entire book devoted to Jack. They wrote one for Matthew, Mark, Luke, and John, but no Jack.

Left to my own devices, I told him there were monsters nearby, waiting to eat him if he behaved badly. If there was a strange sound, I'd say, "Oh, no, the MONSTERS!" and he would immediately turn into a golden child. It was mean, but it also fed his imagination.

I grew to depend on torture to make Jack perform tasks. I think in 16 years, his room was clean three times, by his hand. I never could get him to be tidy. I think he got some sort of "I must live in filth" gene from his father. Now when I look around my clean house, I think "Whew."

Daily torture of Jack began each morning with wake up music. You'd think for a kid who enjoyed Megadeth, you couldn't find something obnoxious-sounding enough to pull him out of his slumber. You'd be wrong. A boy who loves Megadeth very often doesn't fully appreciate Perry Como.

Eventually, people can tune out Perry Como, which is when I pull out yes, show tunes. There is nothing more wonderful to watch than how quickly "Happy Talk" from South Pacific can get a 14-year-old sleeper to the breakfast table. Once he tried to fool me, saying "I don't care if you play that song. In fact, I like it." I said, "Me too." And I began to sing along. This made Jack finish his breakfast AND take out the trash.

To make him move really fast, I chose the most atrocious tunes I could think of at 7 a.m. "The Lonely Goatherd" or "Doe, A Deer" from the Sound of Music, "June is Bustin' Out All Over" from Carousel, "Goin' Courtin'" from Seven Brides for Seven Brothers – these worked well, and they had the added effect of entwining themselves in the listener's brain, sometimes for weeks at a time. One year, everyone in the house ran around singing "The Surry With The Fringe On Top."

Some days I'd say to him "If you get any more tardy slips, I'm playing the Oklahoma soundtrack every morning for the rest of your natural life, and when you move away, I'll call you and play it over the phone and sing along." He'd say, "You have a mean streak, Mom."

Perhaps I was too harsh. Rather than be creative with my less than perfect parenting skills, most of the time, I blew it. I blame my youth, and of course, my parents. If Hitler's parents had been a little nicer during his potty training, perhaps he wouldn't have tried to invade other countries. Sort of makes you think twice about your own ancestry, doesn't it?

Magically, Jack has survived to adulthood, and he could kick butt at a Name that Tune competition.

CAMI

It is funny to me how many names we are assigned in our lifetimes. I was destined to be Jo, coming from a long line of women nicknamed Jo, and it was so firmly established by the advent of Petticoat Junction, that yes, I passed it on to my daughter.

It is a complete wonder that my daughter knows her real name, Cami Jo Erin Roblin. When she first showed up, she looked like the perfect combination of my husband and myself, so we combined our names to call her Cami Jo. It was a good idea at the time, we thought.

My niece, Brittany, calls Cami Jo "Jo-Jo" just like her mother called me Jo-Jo. A legacy! I thought I was too poor to have a legacy.

By the time Cami was 14, she had 22 different nicknames. We started with Bug, because she was cute as one. Then Jo, then Jo Bug, then "The Jo" then Cami, then CJ, then Cjo, then Frap, Frappy Jo, Frappy Po, and Baby Jo. She had several nicknames throughout elementary school, because she was so cute and cuddly, and she had long brown hair and big brown eyes. Some nicknames were unkind, and I really wanted to exploit them here, but she has a mean left hook for a vegetarian, so I can't relate even one funny little story about them, even this one time in first grade. I can only say that it involved chalk.

Anyway, one day my husband remembered reading "Last of the Mohicans" when the father referred to Hawkeye as "my white child." So he started calling Jack and Cami "White boy and White girl" because he had trouble remembering who was who.

Eventually she called herself CeeJay, and her nieces and nephews call her "Aunt Mimi." It's interesting that we never called her Erin, though it is her middle name. Sometimes I still call her Bug.

Then "Mr. Saturday Night" came out, with Billy Crystal doing a routine about his relatives "Indian names" such as Never Buys Retail. My sister and I quickly adopted this practice. Actually, Jeni had an Indian name years before when my cousins dubbed her

"Break-A-Toy." Our kids were now "No Shirt On" and "Brat With A Whine." My husband was "Snores A Lot." I was "Princess Nose In Book."

Jeni calls herself "Bargain Hunter" and her ex-husband had an Indian name involving an unpleasant bodily function. My grandchildren are now "Never Takes A Nap" and "Stands Against The Wall." Never Takes A Nap is also known in the Vanilla Village as "Constant Chatter."

I love that we have all these nicknames. It makes me think we're an ancient people, lyrical by nature, creative and intuitive. Cami used to tap into this when she was a toddler, and she would climb up on a chair to help me dry dishes and put them away, and she would say "God gave me a song. Do you want to hear it?" And I'd say, "Absolutely." She would close her eyes and tilt her head, and sing "I love flowers and trees and little bugs. I love raindrops on the grass. I love a little dirt pile on the porch, and God loves all these things too. Ooo. Ooo. God loves us all too." And I would applaud and cheer wildly. Then I taught her to take a bow. I think it was there where she learned she wanted to be an entertainer.

Chapter 18
VANILLA CUBED—THE GRANDCHILDREN

Taking care of a two and a half year old girl is like sliding down a hill blindfolded, not knowing exactly where the cactus is. I've learned this from the experience of keeping my granddaughter, Cori, for the summer.

Sometimes I wanted to claw at the window and yell "Help, she's destroying my psyche!" Other times, we'd just sit and color.

When I was little, I had dolls that talked when you pulled their string. They would say various sentences and giggle. You could pull their string a hundred times and hear the same five or six cute little sayings. Then your cousins would come along and pull the string too hard and ruin the doll forever.

Once I had a doll that my cousins absolutely destroyed, pushing its eyes in, collapsing an arm, cutting the hair on one side. They didn't pull her string out, though, and she would often say, "I have beautiful eyes, 'cause I eat carrots." She was disillusioned.

I am waiting for my cousins to pull too hard on Cori's string. She has eight stock phrases. "What's your name?" is number one. If you tell her your name, she asks you again within sixty seconds to see if you remember. She checks again within 30 more seconds.

However, if you ask for her name, she will not answer.

"I'm a big girl. I'm growing up." Every day, I mean every hour, no, every other minute, this will be part of the conversation. Sometimes she adds, "I pee in the potty" as proof of growing up. She believes this totally impresses her audience.

"I want to play at the park." At 7 a.m., this is not the request that makes me smile. I'd rather hear, "Let's sleep in 'til noon today," but that just doesn't happen.

"I can do it myself." She says this with her shoes on the wrong feet and her shirt on inside out. "Are you gon bwaid my hair?" she asks while I'm braiding. Her Texas accent makes "hair" a three syllable word.

Stock phrases means she says it over and over and over until it is all you hear in your brain, no matter whether she is in the room.

"Where are we going?" You have just told her three times where you are going, yet as you strap her into the car seat, you hear her ask again. If you choose not to answer, as I have, you hear the question again, then she answers herself and adds, "And don't ask me again." When she does that, it sort of seems like the Twilight Zone.

"I have a owie, I need a bangaid." She is describing a miniscule scratch on her knee, which barely broke the skin three weeks ago, but is apparently the cause of great pain. When a Spongebob Squarepants Band-Aid is applied, said owie is immediately better, for a few minutes until she has to inspect the owie again, studying intently and assessing further damage.

She can't pronounce her "Ls" or "Rs" very well, she's more like Elmer Fudd. I have become an interpreter for those who do not speak "Two."

"You bweve in pwangos?" she asks often. This one took me a long time to decipher. It really means "Do you believe in angels?" She wants to know, because somehow, for some unfathomable reason, she has identified strongly with the movie, "Angels in the Outfield." She knows it by heart. It is her favorite video. She has developed this vanillaism from her great-grandfather.

She asks various people if they bweve in pwangos. At first I thought it sounded like Do you breathe pencils, and then perhaps Do you believe in pretzels, but neither of those could have been right. It took a trip to the video store. I heard her ask it when she saw the tape. It was like I had discovered a new language. I jumped up and down like a game show contestant. "I got it. Angels. Cool." Yes, I do believe in angels. I believe I had one in my apartment for the summer. A talkative one, with a twisted halo.

I thank God for all of these Vanilla souls. What a precious gift, to share the earth with them.

Chapter 19
THE MEANING OF TWISTED

You may have wondered about the title of my column, TWISTED THOUGHTS. Sometimes the thoughts don't twist so far. Then again, sometimes you may wonder, "Where are the men in white coats?"

Twisted thoughts are bits of twisted humor that jump into my brain at random and remain there until I splat them out on paper.

Twisted humor is developed by taking all the pain and embarrassment and anger and complete despair in my world and mixing it with a lot of Kraft Velveeta cheese in the microwave and slapping it between two slices of white bread, adding a drop of vanilla extract and wadding it up and chewing it with bad teeth and spitting it out on the floor in front of the preacher and saying, "Oh, sorry. It must be a tumor."

People ask, how did you get so twisted? I tell them I snorted too much Nestle's Quik in the 60's.

Snort is such a fun word. Say it five times. Say it to someone's face. Say "SNORT" loudly to your boss during a quiet moment at a Board meeting, and make milk come out of his nose. That is the essence of good comedy. And what are they going to do, fire you? For saying Snort? If they do, put it on your resume.

Now say "nougat." Say it slowly in front of the mirror and watch how your mouth moves. Nougat. It makes you smile.

The study of words is fascinating. If I could stand to go back to school, I might study words and become some sort of word doctor.

I did not like school, Sam I am. Not enough laughs there on a daily basis. A kid laughs about 3000 times in a day. Adults laugh about six times in a day. What happened to those 2994 laughs? School. **S**ystematic **C**urtailment **H**appening **O**f **O**ur **L**aughter.

Laughing is better than cheesecake. Laughing so hard you ache, or laughing right after you've cried hard, these are moments for which we all live. Fuji moments. Then twisting the laugh is just taking the joke a step further and falling off the cliff.

I often think of my family when I want a twisted laugh. I'm not being cruel. They're that funny.

My dad never sneezed saying "Achoo." He always says "Ahhhpigfeathers," or "Baahrleycorn." Interestingly, none of his children have sought therapy.

Did you ever run your toe into the corner of the wall and try not to cuss. It's nearly impossible. You don't want to cuss in front of my mom, though. It's like doing the cha-cha at church. It simply isn't done. But one day I stubbed my toe.

Out of my mouth escaped the "S" word. I was hopping and trying to hold on to my toe and cry, and my mother stood there, hands on hips, the death of her middle child on her mind, I'm sure. She said, "If yeew want to talk dirty, why don't y'all just jump up on the table and yell Nasty Word, Nasty Word?"

This immediately struck me so funny, I was crying and laughing and imagining a Broadway show in which 50 or 60 dancers get up on tables and yell "Nasty Word, Nasty Word." Then one of them would start sneezing, "UHHHBARleycorn."

Chapter 20
TWISTED GRAMMAR THOUGHTS

I am a word person. I obsess on words. When people talk, I see the words they are saying, like a ticker-tape above their heads. Some people are quite articulate, and some misspell when they speak. Spelling and grammar mistakes should be punishable by dismemberment, don't you think?

I am always in search of words to live by. I need a new motto every other day or so. Here are some of my favorite pieces of wisdom, extraordinary quotes, from a lifetime of watching TV.

"Those who dance are considered insane by those who can't hear the music."

"The straightest line between a short distance is two points."

"If you can't say something nice about somebody, come sit by me."

"Unable to function as plants, we must serve as manure."

"It's always something."

"There are no times that don't have moments like these."

"Who could it be that makes us naughty? Could it be Satan?"

"Marry a man that smells good."

"You have no power here. Be gone, before someone drops a house on you."

"As if."

"Wouldn't you agree that you like to argue?" "I suddenly awoke with the biggest thighs in Christendom."

"I'm your Huckleberry."

"It's alarming how charming I feel."

If you can quickly recall these quotes when you want to spend time with your kids and all they want to do is watch WWF wrestling, you may sink into your psyche to escape torture. Recently, though, I found a way to watch WWF with my son, with the sound off. Instead of ringside noise, I have a cassette of Scott Joplin ragtime music, and somehow, it looks as though the wrestlers are moving and fighting in time to the piano. I have never enjoyed wrestling until this discovery. And it proves that sometimes, a lack of words is a beautiful thing.

Consider Chaplin movies. Words would ruin them. In Modern Times, when he's roller-skating blindfolded, it is hard to take a breath, much less speak.

While I love words, I am not wordy. I barely talk. I hardly ever talk on the phone and I've been lucky to interview talkative people. I am the quiet one that you have to worry about.

Mostly, I quip. I am the one who makes the whole room laugh with a couple of words, after someone rants. I am also the one who gets in trouble for that.

One time in school, my class discussed stay-at-home moms vs. working women. All the arguments pro and con were played out with the teacher advocating for stay at home types and some aggressive girls arguing for working women, and arguing loudly. Everyone was exhausted. The teacher finally asked who was to blame for the whole mess. From the back of the room, I yelled, "Your mother." I didn't get good grades.

Some folks don't need words the way I do. Beautiful supermodels tend to have fewer words in play than those who tend not to be beautiful. Why is that? Is beauty lofty? We seem to give more credit to a beautiful blonde than a fat girl with fuzzy hair even if the chubby one is more articulate and intelligent. I personally think that the problem for blondes is that all the words are concealed in what we call books.

Men don't seem to need as many words, either. Not that they would understand as many. They seem to exist in the grunt world, where women have graduated from the cave. Men can achieve more with fewer words, where a woman would have to justify every move with a paragraph.

Choose Your Words Wisely

I have come to you in the past to ask that you not use quote marks in the air, nor mispronounce nuclear, library and data. Now I must come to you again and let you know that just because you might know some big words, it is not necessary to enlighten us all regarding your vast vocabulary.

Get permission from a true wordsmith prior to using the word "edifice" or "augment." Never say "let me just say." This is a cardinal rule. A license must be obtained for the usage of more than four multi-syllabic words per sentence.

Currently, only Dennis Miller, William F. Buckley, and George Carlin hold these licenses. This is for good reason. Language is an art. Art is entertainment. If you are saying words too big for your IQ just to impress someone, you ain't entertaining anyone.

In writing, please remember to limit sentences to less than 30 words. A sentence should not be a paragraph. Eliminate the word "that" whenever and wherever possible. Take out "You" and "I" statements unless absolutely necessary.

You have heard about double negatives. There don't seem to be no reasons to use them. This also applies to double positives, such as "In addition, I also."

A preposition is a word you shouldn't end a sentence with. Uncle Rex tells us, "A young boy says to his Dad, about to read a story,

'How come you brought that book I didn't want to be read to out of up for'?"

Worth mentioning again, never use the phrase "Enclosed please find…" If it's enclosed, I'll find it. Never use "regards" – you only get one. There are nine famous reindeer, not reindeers. It's the same with sheep, although they don't get the fame the reindeer get.

Also, no one cares about "paradigms." Stop saying that word. Don't get caught up in cliché phrases, such as "focus area" or "cultural needs" or "planning matrix." The bottom line is we don't like the phrase, "It's all about the bottom line."

If your writing reflects such mistakes, it's a cinch your speech could be cleaned up. In Willows, and not because we have to, we use smaller words. We like clear, concise messages decorated with sharp humor. We would eschew obfuscation (stop making things difficult to understand). We despise sesquipedalians (people who tend to use big words all the time).

Here's a helpful hint. If yours is the only voice heard for the last 20 minutes, you have already bored everyone and someone sitting nearby is seriously thinking about using their pencil as a weapon. Put that in the back of your mind as you wax philosophic. Grandma put it more bluntly. "You have the floor, now don't pee on it."

Twisty Word Woman Strikes Again

"Like" is a funny word. In the American Heritage dictionary, it has ten similar or like meanings, including 1) To find pleasant: "I like you"; 2) To want, wish or prefer: "The lady would like a beer"; 3) To be fond of, as in preferences: "I'd like a Heineken"; 4) Similar: "I'd like the same"; 5) In the typical manner of: "That's not like you"; 6) Disposed to: "feel like drinking"; 7) Indicative of : "Looks like Miller time"; 8) Equivalent or as if: "He drank like crazy"; 9) In the same way: "Tell it like it is"; and 10) Resembling or characteristic of: "Act like a lady."

The dictionary goes on to give a list of similar or like words, called synonyms: Alike, analogous, comparable, corresponding, equivalent, parallel, and uniform. These words all seem the same to me.

This particular dictionary goes on to tell the story of As vs. Like, the continuing controversy. "Like" has been used as a conjunction since Shakespeare's time by the best writers. The usage has come under heavy fire from purists, so much so that the word is best avoided on grounds of prudence. So, we say "Winston tastes good, as a cigarette should, rather than like it should, which is why cigarettes are not advertised on network TV, whose producers are appalled at grammatical errors with regard to tobacco.

You have to be careful with likewise, too. Since likewise is not a conjunction, it cannot take the place of and, as in "He dropped his money, likewise, his bottle of bourbon." A better sentence would be, "He was walking around in a drunken stupor."

Even so, the likelihood of like-minded folks writing about lilacs is not likely, although the likeness of one lilac is like another. Lilacs are not fungi, so to liken them to lichen is just wrong.

All manner of things and people are likeable, including lollipops, which are also lickable.

Like is also a great slang word. Like you didn't know that. Like, what is this fascination with one word? Are you like weirding out? What is that like? Does Sally Field know what people really, really like?

It can be a whole conversation among those who grew up in the 60s – likeminded folks. "Like, what it is, man."

"Like, yeah."

"Hey, like this stuff is really cool."

"Like wow, man."

"I'm liking this."

"It's like nothing else."

"I like Ike."

"Tina's pretty cool, too, man."

Incidentally, the campaign slogan for Eisenhower, "I like Ike" was frought with nail-biting indecisiveness. Other slogans suggested were "Dwight is Dright One" and "Shower with Eisenhower" and "Stevenson Sucks" and "Best Bald Guy Wins."

People used to say "Like it or lump it." This was replaced by "Like it or leave it" which led to "Like it or Not," which led to "Not," which is often accompanied by the hand in a stop sign position, and "Talk to the hand because the face ain't listening." That is for when you don't like what you hear.

People often say they love something when the emotion they truly feel is extreme like. The degrees of like vary like mad, for instance, I like spinach and I like rocky road ice cream, but I wouldn't care to substitute one for the other.

My family members say they like something when they really mean they can't stand it. Suppose a young child is screaming his head off in public, and the guardian of said child is doing nothing about it. Mom would say, "Oh, I like that." Another family member would say, "Give me five minutes with that kid, I'd like that." Yet another relative would say, "I'd like five minutes with the mother." Another family member (probably me) would say, "I'd like to get out of here and go get a beer."

There's the old joke, "How do you like your eggs?" "I like them fine." There's the new cop language for like, "The guy with the spiked hair, we like him for burglary." That means he is the likely suspect.

Like it or not, I'm done with "LIKE" unless you'd like something else.

A Grammar Queen Sermon

Some words should just be outlawed. I should know. I've heard them all. I write down each one that I've heard more than three times in the same half-hour, and folks, no one around here is doing that "choosing one's words wisely" thing.

There is a word, actually several, I imagine, for pompous speechmaking. The one I'm thinking of is grandiloquence, of which a few Willows folks are guilty, so let me preach the grammar queen gospel.

I attended a 30-minute meeting in which the word "cogent" and a form of the word, "cogency" were used more than six times. Cogent means "forcefully convincing." I am convinced I never want to hear it in any form.

Basically, I am opposed to being drowned by another person's vocabulary or semblance thereof. Don't try to impress me with your speech, it makes me homicidal.

If you learn nothing else from me, remember this: Do not use a noun as a verb. For instance, "umbrella" is a noun, meaning a device for sun or rain protection. An idea is not am umbrella. An idea does not umbrella. You may have an idea that you need an umbrella, if raindrops keep falling on your head, but if it is raining and you are using an umbrella, you are not umbrella-ing. An idea can encompass, but it is hardly wetness protection.

Generally, "J" words with more than three syllables only serve to irritate others. "Juxtaposition" means to place items side by side, but when a speaker says "juxtaposition" more than once, I want to place a sharp object next to their dull brain. Some "P" words have the same effect, such as "pejorative" and "perspicacity." Impress me only once with your "P."

Latin is not taught in school anymore, and speakers who use Latin phrases are merely showing their age or quoting their mom. No more cliché "caveat emptor," "veni, vidi, vici," or "carpe diem," please. No more "ad hominem" or "ad infinitum." I've heard it ad nauseum.

Also, if you don't know the meaning of the word, please don't impress me that you know how to pronounce it. My grandson could, at age 2, recite the Star Trek prologue which begins, "Space, the final frontier..." but it's only cute when he does it – my Dad knows the words too, but he doesn't have the same dazzling effect.

Another word we can outlaw is "brouhaha." It means "uproar." Can't we just say uproar? When I hear brouhaha, I want to giggle, "Ha ha ha." I am troubled by the word "onerous." I cannot connect to someone who uses the word "nexus." I get agitated when I hear "dither." I think it is exceptionally bad to say "atrocity." I feel sad to a ridiculous degree when I hear "lugubrious." If your speech is peppered with these types of words, it is obvious that when you were in third grade, you got in a lot of fights on the playground.

My biggest peeve, not even a pet.... Remember one regard and one toward per person. Stop saying "in regards to" and "towards that end." Stop it, I say. You only get ONE.

You may think this is harsh. I don't care. Good grammar and spelling mean the world to me, despite my being a journalist. I know its sick, but I can't go to the supermarket if the shopping list has a misspelled word. I can't walk into the 98 cent store, because there is a sign out front that reads "Humungus values." I can't eat in a restaurant with mistakes on the menu. I become completely frazzled when I see people talking, using words I know they can't spell. I see the words they speak, as though a ticker-tape is running above their heads. It's a proverbial word jungle out there, and I am alone in the thick of it, watching your grammar. It is my mission.

More Wrath from the Grammar Queen

Ok, I've heard enough. The primary election is over, and still, I have received at least four political advertisements in the last week, with improper grammar and even misspelled words, along with their slung mud.

This propaganda is freely distributed to the general public with the intent to make us even more stupid. They think we're all looking at the mail saying, "Huh, garsh, Edna! This fella uses those real BIG words. We oughta vote fer him."

People, if you are reading the commercial slop still spewing from your local politician, please take a good long look at what your brain is receiving. Stop waving your flags long enough to look at your English books. You're all becoming too symbol-minded.

Politicians, put some thought into your ads, and take the time to look up some of the bigger words. They may not mean what you think. Don't go for fancy. Aim for accuracy. Actually, stop writing about it altogether and go do what you said you were going to do if elected. And take me off your mailing list.

Here are 10 of your most common oral and written hideous errors. First, you keep talking about "first annual" reports or celebrations or meetings. STOP. You can have a first, and you can have an annual, but you cannot have a first annual. When you have a second, then you can have a second annual. Until then, there's only been one. Let the logic seep in.

Second, please stop writing "enclosed please find." If it's enclosed, I'll find it. Third, never say "thus" again. Thou art not Shakespeare. Fourth, get a life, not a lifestyle. Very few people can afford to style their lives.

Fifth, don't talk to me about "glitches." What an ugly word. It makes people shudder, like nails on a chalkboard.

Sixth, there is a difference between comprise and compose. Compose means to create or put together. Comprise means to contain or include. Use each word sparingly. In Willows, use "made up of" but don't put "of" at the end of the sentence.

Seventh, let's talk about choices. You make a choice "between" two things and "among" more than two things.

Eighth, to accept means to receive. Except means to exclude. You do not "except" food stamps. You do not make an "acception" to the rules. Not even in Willows.

Ninth, you keep writing and saying "over" when you mean "more than." Stop. Over is a direction, as in "over-easy." More than refers to numbers. Don't say "I have over $300" or I will come over there and give you more than one grammar-shaking fist.

Finally, remember the English teacher's last words, "If you dangle your participle, I'll split your infinitive."

A few more gripes from the past—Those quotation marks in the air are SO disgusting. Do me a favor and don't quote anyone. Make up your own clever remarks.

Once again, REGARD, TOWARD. No "S."

Learn how to pronounce "nuclear," "data," "library," "idea" and "mirror." Find a "Hick to English" guide and practice.

Chapter 21
TWISTED YET POETIC EDUCATION

Spend Some Time Inside My Brain
I've been thinking a lot about time, lately. Mostly because there aren't enough hours in the day. And my commute time takes forever. I need a few moments for myself.

My time is valuable. Can I have a few minutes of your time? I don't have any time. Time is up. Downtime. Time is on my side. Do you have a second? Do you have a minute? Can we have a moment of silence? It is a momentous occasion.

Idle time and trouble go hand in hand. Please hold. I want to hold your hand. Hand it over. Overtime. (You thought I got off track, didn't you?) I've asked you time and time again. Time after time. Maybe this time you'll listen. Time is ticking. Like sands through the hourglass, so are the days of our lives. Having the time of our lives. Once in a lifetime. Do you read Time and Life? The life and times of Judge Roy Bean. Boston Beans. Bean Dip. Chips & Dip. Dip stick. Stick in the mud. Stuck…Stuck in the middle. My watch is stuck at 2:30. (Back again.) I'd hate to be stuck in the Middle Ages. The clock struck one. Midstroke. Stroke of midnight. Midnight on the oasis. (One question. If midnight is the bewitching hour, then why was Bewitched on Thursday nights in primetime, and what did they do to the real Darrin?)

The zero hour. The children's hour. Play time. Break time. Time to break up. Time to move on. On time. Time off. Vacation time. Killing time. Be a faithful steward of time, talent and money. One thing at a time. One day at a time. Time marches on. What time is it?

Time to hit the road. Time will tell. William Tell. Can you tell time? Is it time to eat yet? Are you done eating? What time is suppertime in summertime? Did you clean your plate? Time to do dishes.

Sometime I'd like to discuss it. Take time to talk. Talk to the hand. It's like talking to a wall. The clock on the wall is faster than the clock in the hall.

Beat the clock. Put an egg in your shoe and beat it. The time is now. Time waits for no one. Don't ask for whom the bell tolls. It tolls for thee. Toll house cookies take only a few minutes to bake. Shake & Bake time. Gotta make time. Time's running out. Out of time.

Up to date. Up to snuff. Snuff it out. In and out. Around the corner. Cornerstone of time. Time to run. Time for fun. Don't spend too much time in the sun.

Take a trip down memory lane. Time to remember the days of September. Time for school. Don't be late. I'm late for a very important date. Take time to date before marriage. Take a week off. Take up to six months to pay. Take a year to decide. Take your time.

Don't waste your time. Look what time has done to your waist. Time to exercise. Exercise your rights. Do you have the right time? Have I caught you at a bad time? "Good Times" was a great showcase for the talents of Jimmie Walker.

I go out walkin' after midnight. Night time is the right time. Meet me on time. Meet me in St. Louis, Louis. Meetings like this take up a lot of my time. Taking up time and space. What time is it in space? In the space of two minutes, I could sell you a car.

Driving time is an hour and ten minutes. Minute men often took their time. It only takes 48 seconds to make Minute Maid orange juice. OJ's trial took the longest time! Time trials determine pole position.

If the big hand is on the 12 and the little hand is on the 6, it is time to go to lunch. Thank God I had the time to tell you. I'm so glad we had this time together, just to have a laugh and sing a song. Seems we just get started and before you know it, comes the time we have to say so long.

Inspired by Sondheim...to the Class of 2002

Into the world you now must go, you have your shot, your one free throw,

Into the world, don't make a mess – You must be on your journey.

Into the world, a quest for growth, a test of all that you are worth,

Into the world, but come back soon, and don't forget your laundry.

The way is clear. The car is in gear...Get out of here, and get your education.

Whether you work or go to school, or if you do both, there is one rule.

Keep a clear head and sit up straight. Make sure you pay attention.

Into the world we let you go, we hope you know the way to go.

Into the world no longer a kid, you have a destination.

Your future's so bright, wear sunglasses at night. Take charge of your life, and do it right.

Into the world, you're on your own. You once were small but now you're grown.

Into the world, you're on your way. Don't forget to seize each day.

Into the world to start a new life, While your parents start medication.

Into the world, you're just eighteen, kind of green, but kind of mean

Into the world we promised you – it's full of education.

The path is clear. So have no fear. Go forth and study four more years.

Into the world you've got to go, You're eager to run, you've got to know

What in the world is out there for you...You must be on your journey.

Into the world, into the world, into the world, and home before dark.

Well, maybe not. But call us when you get there.

Listen and Repeat

Do you know what kind of learner you are? Most people learn visually, which is why school works, and why people read newspapers.

Some people, however, and my family is full of 'em, learn auditorily, which would explain why we're a bunch of gossips.

School very often doesn't work for those who learn auditorily. It is unfortunate, because these people are often the brightest crayons in the box. Only certain subjects are taught to the ear. Foreign language, for example. In French class, you hear, "Ecote et repete" which means "listen and repeat." You don't get this in your English class. You get repetitive sentence writing – a visual tool.

As Walt Disney knew ages ago, if you hear something in rhyme or song, you learn it quickly. That's why we, the class of '76 and prior, all heard our times tables as sung by Jiminy Cricket. They don't do that in school anymore. Ain't it a shame?

I am teaching my grandchildren great literature. They don't give a crap about it, unless I start talking funny, because they are fourth generation auditory learners. Or stubborn. So I tell them stories with my tongue stuck under my top teeth, or with a heavy southern accent.

Imagine epic poems done this way, and you will begin to appreciate them. The Wreck of the Hesperus with a lisp. Hiawatha from deep in the heart of Texas. Story time is awesome at my house. Did I ever tell you the story of Gertrude? This is a tongue under the teeth thing. Try it.

Once upon a time, I was very young. I used to play hard all day. One day, I went over the hill to play, and I played and I played all day, and I got so very tired. So I came back over the hill to home, and there was my father, and there was my mother, and there was my sister, but WHERE was my baby brother? Gertrude had eaten him.

I was SO MAD, I could have thrown rocks, but Gertrude was my friend, so I forgave her.

The next day, I went over the hill to play, and I played and I played all day, and got so very tired. I came back over the hill to home, and there was my father, and there was my mother, but WHERE was my sister? Gertrude had eaten her.

I was SO MAD, I could have pitched a hissy fit, but Gertrude was my friend, so I forgave her.

The next day, I went over the hill to play, and I played and I played all day and I got so very tired, that I came back over the hill to home, and there was my father. But WHERE was my mother? Gertrude had eaten her, too.

I was SO MAD, I could have spit nails. But Gertrude was my friend, so I forgave her. But I gave her a stern look.

The next day, I went over the hill to play, and I played and I played all day. I got so very tired and I came back over the hill to home. WHERE was my father? Gertrude had eaten him, too.

I was SO MAD I saw flames. But Gertrude was my friend, so I forgave her.

The next day, I went over the hill to play, and I played and I played all day and I got very, very tired. So I came back over the hill to home, and there was my father, and there was my mother, and there was my sister, and there was my little baby brother, Herman.

Gertrude had burped.

The problem with telling a story with your tongue under your teeth is that you feel so silly and you continue to talk that way long after the story is over. Don't do it before dinner, or you'll be ordering a pizza with a speech impediment.

Some of the most pleasurable words to say with your tongue under your teeth are: chicken sandwiches, post-nasal drip, marshmallows, bubblegum, and County Supervisor.

The other night I tried to help my daughter memorize part of Julius Caesar, and it was great fun saying "Friends, Romans, Countrymen..." with my tongue stuck in place. It was even better with a southern accent. I was thinking how much longer the Roman Empire would have lasted, had they an outrageous, outspoken Texan for a leader.

Tongue Twisted Thoughts

One of the best games to play in the car if you travel with your family (a practice I do not recommend) is "Who Can Say the Best Tongue Twister?"

You say you know Peter Piper, the Wood Chuck, Sue, the seller of Sea Shells, the Baby Buggy Bumpers? Amateur. I, however, am elevated to professional twister status because I was able to read "Fox in Sox" by Dr. Seuss at age 3.

Try this Sick Sheep story on your next sojourn to Saskatchewan:

The slick sixth sheik's sixth son's sixth sheep is sick, so they slipped the sheep some secret serum, stirring in some sort of sappy syrup supposedly secured by Sammy the skinny slimy snake. Suddenly, the sheik's sixth son's sixth sheep, Cicely, succumbed.

Sheik Sol, sixth son Stuart, and Sammy the snake shouted swearwords to the sky. "Somebody start CPR," sobbed Stuart. Stuart sought solace in shots of Schnapps. Sad and sullen, Sammy sold his stocks and set sail for Sacramento. "See ya, Sol," said Sammy. "Cheerio," shouted Sheik Sol.

Several solid citizens suffered and sorrowed with Sheik Sol and his sixth son Stuart at Summerset Sheep Cemetery. Citizens Supporting Sick Sheep (CSSS) staged a show celebrating sheep sisterhood.

Somehow, sorrowful Stuart stayed suicidal, spurning support. Sheik Sol said, "Shame." Stuart's sister, Sue, sought State assistance, saying Stuart should receive stipends. State supervisors shunned Sue, saying sheiks sons assert substantial assets and significant securities, so Stuart should stay sober.

Sheepless Stuart sobbed. Sister Sue seemed subdued. She said, "I shall sell seashells by the seashore!" "Go sell sea shells, Sister Sue," said Stuart, "see if someone stresses." Sue stomped, saying "Sarcasm sucks, Stu."

"Shove off, Sue," said Stuart.

Sometime subsequently, Sheik Sol secured six salmon, saying "Stuart, start supper."

"Sure, sire," said Stuart. The sizzling salmon supper satisfied Sol and Stuart sufficiently. Still Stuart said snidely, "Sleep soundly? Oh sure." Sheik Sol said, "Son, sip a sedative."

Some of Sol's subjects said a statue of Cicely should stand in the center of Sheik Sol's sheep sanctuary. "Certainly," said Stuart, who sent for Steve Simmons, Chief Sheep Sculptor. Several citizens searched for Steve simultaneously, in sheep shearing stations and certain sculpting spots.

Suddenly, Chief Sheep Sculptor Steve Simmons stepped up. Slobbering on Steve's shoulder, Stuart stated the status of the sheep situation, sobbing "Sweet Cicely."

Sadly, Steve Simmons said "Since 66, sheep sculpting sorta subsided, so Stuart should seek similar statues of assorted substances. Essentially, Steve said, "Stuff Cicely."

So then, townsfolk tried taxidermy, but that's another story. A scintillating sequel. See you soon.

Ode to 1999

Oh, Good old 1999, the year has been a banner.

The lovely stories and pictures of wrecks and things heard on the police scanner.

For me it all began in March, when I was hired by Dave.

"I'd love to write," I said to him, "to quality I am a slave."

"I'd love to drive for miles and miles to cover a council meeting."

Make sure to get the councilmen's names right, Dave warned, for their fame is fleeting.

Then April came and with the spring, my coverage of school board conventions.

What joy, what FUN, let's all stay past bedtime to discuss the Board's intentions.

Then Lamb Derby and graduation came with all their pomp and circumstance.

There was a great parade, the Honker band played on the courthouse steps and danced.

Elizabeth the Editor was introduced one day, then we got brand new iMacs.

We made the leap from manual to digital and from sundials to Timex.

"The paper's looking better," everyone said, "And its all because of you."

"Yeah, I did that," I said because I give credit where it is due.

The advent of computers and digital cameras and spell check was quite helpful.

But mostly the people just want to read what I write, in fact they have a shelf full.

I'm only kidding, folks, its just a joke. My ego is not that conspicuous.

But I don't mind a fan or two. In fact to them, I'm assiduous. (Look it up.)

Every day we write and write and talk to many interesting folks.

We go to meetings, take pictures on the street, and think up clever jokes.

Carefully we craft our stories and stick them on the press.

Then we cross our fingers, kick the machine, and pray for God to bless.

A new decade, century and millennium are just around the bend,

But we'll still be here at least one more year, on that you can depend.

We'll keep bringing you the news and ads and pictures of your neighbors.

And you'll keep giving us words to write by your tremendous behaviors.

This poem is short, I fear, because I'm all undone.

But I leave you quoting Dickens, "God Bless Us, Every One."

Peeve Poem

I love Dr. Seuss. He's of such great use. Since my grandson turned two, practically all we do is turn page after page reading Horton Hears a Who.

So I dedicate this writing to a space alien sighting and bad poetry with no class. If you think it mundane or perhaps think me insane, well, I'll pray for you when I attend mass.

I have a list of you people who've angered me so much I've longed for a tower and a gun. Though it isn't PMS, it isn't hard to take a guess that if I had a Smith & Wesson, I'd have fun.

On the top of the list, my peeves regarding your speech. The number one error, just out of my reach. Folks, nuclear is pronounced as it is spelled. I hear it said wrong and I yell, "If you say nuke-u-lar, I will go for your jugular!

More additions to my list include: those who chew tobacco, it's just so rude. Well, maybe it's not rude to chew, but it sure makes me sick when I see people spew. Next, people who scrape their forks on their plates; people who have bad personality traits; people who ask for a tissue, please, and before you get back end up using their sleeve. Actually no one would cheer and whistle at folks using irregular methods of snot dismissal.

Next, people who write for the IRS, they tend to write more when they should write much less. Then people who ask, "Is it hot enough for you?" when it's so blasted hot you turn into glue. And people who ask "Are you working hard or hardly working?" like they wrote that themselves—this leaves me smirking. They believe it's so funny they throw their heads back and laugh, well; it hasn't been funny since I was two and a half.

Men named Dale, Duane or Ralph should really be spanked. I've met quite a few and they're usually tanked. People who smile at Monday morning meetings should all get in line for their Monday night beatings. And if you go to a meeting and act like big jerks, expect your name in the paper. That's how it works.

If you own a monster truck with tires big as a moose, don't drive like a maniac and we'll call a truce. If you drive really slow on I-5 everyday, God will get you for that in his own special way. Driving with your blinker on irritates my soul. Pay attention, turn it off, or you'll have to pay the toll. Drive like you're going straight to heaven, though odds are its Wal-Mart or Seven-Eleven.

You already know the right words to say. I've told you about "liberry" and "data" and by the way, those quote marks in the air with your fingers, no one does it much but the image still lingers. I've told you about etiquette on the phone, be brief, concise and use a non-perky tone. Tell me who's calling and make it simple—do it right from now on or God will give you a pimple.

Show me pictures of your family, and I'll show you mine. It's only fair – you started it. You have no right to whine. If you buy me ice cream, though, I'll look through your photo books, and I'll say its obvious where your children got their looks.

All of the above people must be ashamed. That's why I wrote this. They're all to be blamed. To get back at these people, each one of the nuts, I see them in chairs much too small for their butts. Then I draw in a big breath and with all of my power, I sit before them and start name-calling for hours. I start with the wonderful insult, "YOU BIG." and then list a few names that would curl a straight wig. "You Big" sounds like four syllables, long and drawn out – then squint your eyes while words pour out your spout.

I'd like to sit and rhyme all day, but there are articles to write. And some would say to make my pay, this poetry is too light. So to all of you who love this goo, be happy and goodnight.

Chapter 22
TWISTED DRIVING THOUGHTS

Hunk O Junk

I have a love/hate relationship with my car right now. It was doing so well, commuting hundreds of miles each week on sips of oil and daily tankfuls of gas, avoiding roadkill and highway patrol officers left and right. Then came the Terror of Tuesday, a day that will live in infamy, at least in my estimation.

Driving happily along, the little blue car started jerking forward, as though the gas pedal wasn't floored. Concerned, I slowed down just a bit, and it went zip, zip, jerk jerk jerk, zip zip. Then the most horrendous noise in the world began. If you've ever been in front of a speeding semi, braking to avoid rear-ending your tiny car, you would know the noise. With my little Hyundai, though, the noise came from under my feet. I thought it might fall apart and I would suddenly be left with a Flintstone car. Then it began to shake and groan a twisted metal groan. It was unhappy. I was not in the best mood, either.

I was two orchards away from a phone booth. I stopped the car and tried to start it again. It yelled at me that it didn't care to continue. It had gone far enough.

Wearing black, I suddenly found myself mourning the loss of my Excel. Not fond of walking, my loss was profound and deeply heartfelt, not to mention whiny.

Stranded. Abandoned by my own transportation. Agony set in as my wallet poured out money for towing. When I was good and depressed, I got a call from the mechanic to let me know the price to pay for further mobilization. Suicide became a viable alternative. Who wants to be a millionaire? Me. But no, I'm a journalist.

People used to ask me what kind of car I drove. I answered, "Blue." Now I know what 'ol Blue sounds like when the transmission gives out. I know more about it than I ever cared to know. And I know it takes almost 10 days of repentance before another transmission is put in and ready to drive. Oh, how to appreciate your transportation – go without it for 10 days. You begin to feel foolish, asking for rides.

People with well-running cars told me, "Oh, that's too bad about your car." They feel my pain. They offer me rides around town, and I envy their hands on their steering wheels.

Actually, I want to thank the guys who stopped on Highway 45 to let me use a cell phone. That was so nice. I appreciate everyone who has helped in my time of sorrow.

I kind of wish for the days of the old west right now, because then I could ride a horse to work. Horses don't drop their transmissions, and you don't have to fill them with oil. I bet you couldn't run them more than 800 miles per week though. They would trot their hooves off.

I don't skateboard, I don't have a bike, and neither method is acceptable for a long commute...I just cant see myself in anything but 'ol Blue. I am eternally grateful to the mechanical wizards at Wunsch, and so glad to be on the road again – It's Hi yo Hyundai, away!

You Drive Me Crazy!

Disclaimer: This is a humor column, meant to offend everyone equally. Do not feel left out if you were not offended. I will get to you later.

I drive a lot, and I have seen some atrocious behavior. I have even tried some atrocious driving behavior, but I do not get away with it like y'all do. There seems to be an immediate signal from the guilt center of my soul to the dispatch at CHP. I cannot go 75 on the freeway without several people passing me and flipping me off for going so slow, so I speed up to 80, and the bright lights are suddenly pulling me over.

One time I got out of a ticket because I pointed out to the officer that the cars passing the scene of me being pulled over were, in fact, approaching the speed of light. Some country roads around here were built for land speed records, but you needn't leave your blinker on, no matter how far into the future you may feel the need to turn.

Willows folks apparently think of Airport Road as a temporal flux in space and time, across from Wal-Mart. Yes, in Willows it appears that shopping at Wal-Mart is the equivalent of losing a few brain cells to drug use, because people who drive out of their parking lot seem to have had their basic skills sapped.

Drivers leaving the lot can clearly see a stop sign directly across the street from them; it is a tall pole with an octagonal red sign which reads "STOP." Cars have been seen idling at this place, their right turn indicators blinking away, indicating a desire to turn right.

The shopper apparently believes this vision to be a figment of the imagination, because there is no hesitation on his part to cross traffic, yes, CROSS TRAFFIC, to turn left, directly in front of the person at the stop sign.

There is a well known and often studied handbook, called, ironically, the "California Driver's Handbook." This guide can be obtained at the Department of Motor Vehicles, where we can study it while standing in line. In fact, to obtain a driver's license, Californians are sometimes required to possess some of the knowledge in the book. Oddly enough, books are quite often a source of helpful information.

There is a small portion of the California Driver's Handbook I'd like to point out. It says DO NOT cross a traffic lane to make a turn when you don't have the right of way. Let me 'splain it to you, Lucy. STOP TRYING TO KILL ME. People have been turning in front of me for two years now. STOP IT.

For instance, did you know that drivers are required to slow down and pull over to the right of the road when an emergency vehicle is coming along, sirens blaring? Its true! Oh, and when there is a crossroad between your car and the emergency vehicle, you are not only required to slow down, but actually stop. Am I the only one who does this? Am I the only one who retained any sort of knowledge from Driver's Ed.?

Ok, granted, I cannot remember which way to turn my wheels when parking on a hill, however, if there is hill parking in Glenn County, I have not been affected. And when in San Francisco, I do as the Romans do, and turn my wheels the same way as everyone else.

This is called logic, or USING COMMON SENSE, a rare practice on California roads.

It would be logical, for instance, to slow down in the rain. Driving fast does not make the rain slow down or get you to your destination any safer or drier, no matter what cartoon you may have witnessed.

Also, don't pass without enough room, and don't pass on the right. You could be running someone IMPORTANT off the road.

Are you constantly passing people, to the point where you need a support group to deal with it? Here's the way to tell if you're obsessed with passing. Look in your rear view mirror. If the people you just passed are applauding you, it is likely sarcasm. Stop trying to be the first car. You are not. The first car is way ahead of you.

Generally, people in Glenn County drive well on sunny days, when there are few people on the road. Factor in darkness, rain, a car ahead of them, and drivers start to lose it.

"Aaauuuggghhhh! What'll I do? It's dark out there! – I know, I'll make my own rules. Forget that handbook jazz."

Oh, and people? The blinkers, also known as turn signals, are used to indicate whether the car will next turn right or left. Turning on the right blinker usually means the car will turn right soon, and the left blinker should indicate that the vehicle will make a left turn. In a perfect world, these turns would be made from the TURN LANE. However, this is not often the case.

Would that we could foresee going to Taco Bell, then we could possibly get into the turn lane before it is too late. Sometimes we think about turning in at Taco Bell and even indicate such an idea with the blinkers. Then we change our minds. We forget to inform the rest of the public regarding the change of appetite, and yet we hear horns when no turn is made. Strange isn't it?

So often a person has decided to make that turn, but does not venture into the turn lane, as it would require moving out of the way of those who are not turning. Oh, they slow down, and 50 percent of the time they might flip on the blinker but they refuse to move into the turn lane until the very last moment.

If I am behind them and their window is down, they get an audible explanation of where they ought to have made the turn, as well as a visual aid. I try to be helpful where I can.

Oddly enough, my helpful information is seen as "road rage." Go figure. I just wanted to be the spokesperson for the DMV. "The California Driver's Handbook – Don't Leave Home Without It!"

Reno Accident

That was me in a nasty accident last week. A big rig tried to squeeze into my lane. I was between the truck and a concrete wall. (A truck and a hard place) Traffic was fairly light. There was no one close by when the truck moved closer and closer to me. I swerved, my back wheels locked up, and my little blue Hyundai went sideways and crashed. All I heard was screaming and scraping of metal. That sound will never escape me.

Just a couple thoughts on luck. I apparently have good luck. Mm hmm. I had the misfortune of wrecking my vehicle, but I was lucky because there was only a little blood and no broken bones and the kids are still ok with my driving. I had four teenagers with me and they didn't die, despite the fact that we hit boulders and wrapped the car with a fence and skidded to a stop in the avalanche area just 20 feet short of the fast-flowing Truckee River. No kidding.

I am of the opinion that we would have been lucky had we NOT experienced the crash, and arrived home the day expected. However, this is not the sort of luck I am afforded. I am rather like the three-legged blind and deaf dog named Lucky.

My luck is like this. If I fall down in the snow, I am sure to break a leg, but luckily I don't break both of them, because God is watching out for me. Thanks, God, for our bruises and bumps. It could have been much worse.

I hit the steering wheel while twisting around, and injured my spleen. I also hurt my knee and went temporarily into orbit, incoherent and frantic. Teen #1 received a compressed spine. Teen #2 got a sprained neck and a black eye. Teen #3 suffered a black eye and a bruise from the seat belt. Teen #4 was uninjured until she exited the vehicle and turned to check on the others. Then she bumped her head on the fence surrounding the car.

Luckily, the uninjured teen had the presence of mind to keep the rest of us as calm as possible, putting off her own breakdown for a few hours.

I want to take this opportunity to thank the roadside angels who provided cell phone access to 911, and hands to hold until paramedics arrived. Thank you, wonderful paramedics for your kind assistance and medical knowledge. Thank you, CHP Officer, for telling me I did all the right things.

Thank you, doctors at Tahoe Forest Hospital for the big dose of Percodan. That was extremely helpful and I was lucky to get it before the shock wore off.

Thank you, Mom and Pop, for helping me get a new used car so

I could come back home. What kind of car is it, you ask? It's a pretty white car, with a cup holder.

Thank you, Willows Journal, for your support, and thanks for covering for me while I was recuperating. Thank you readers and friends for your calls and your concern. I appreciate your thoughts and prayers.

I also want to thank each of my girls for wearing their seat belts without being prompted. I think of the old commercial where eggs are strapped into their seats in their egg-mobile. One of them is not seat-belted, and when they crash, he is scrambled. Tamara, Wendi, Jessica and my baby Cami, you all proved yourselves brave and hard-boiled.

Trippin' Down the Road

I've been wondering where certain roads get their names and why other roads are named most inappropriately. Most people don't pay any attention to the names of the streets because they know where they're going. I tend to get lost among the tree streets.

There is usually a Frontage Road near the front of every town near a highway. However, none of these towns have a "Backage Road" on the back side of town. Do people make accidents happen on "causeways" and do people do drugs on "highways" (only on road trips) and why are there tollbooths on "freeways?" Why do we insist on the redundant, "roadway?" Shouldn't Chico's "skyway" be elevated a bit? Why aren't there any carnivals on the fairway? People very rarely drive on a stairway, and you know the old joke about parking on the driveway and driving on the parkway. Parkways ought to all lead to Yellowstone. Driveways ought not to lead into the house.

In England, the streets are called motorways. It seems they should be lined with auto repair shops.

Why do we think its clever to name streets after the alphabet or numbers? In Glenn County, they've run out of single letters and had to double up on the alphabet, as in Road OO and ZZ. That's just silly. Some towns have a First Street, First Avenue and First Drive. None of them were first. The first road is usually Main Street, and Disneyland has a Main Street, USA, which is not a major thoroughfare for driving. By the same token, other USA main streets do not typically offer the best of Disney.

After numbers and letters, the most popular street names are Elm and Maple. Tree streets. And Chico streets spell out the word Chico – Cherry, Hazel, Ivy, Chestnut and Oak. Clever trees. Then there are "region" streets, like Humboldt and Plumas, which cover all of Nevada, California and Arizona. Big regions. Doesn't it gripe you see Sacramento Street 99 miles from Sacramento?

Just once I'd like to see a street named Wonk or Flipsky or Deedle. Wouldn't that make your neighborhood smile? Atlantic City had the right idea, naming their streets after Monopoly boards. Butte City is unique, giving all three of their streets Irish names. The "city" itself is unique, as it boasts of a mint green building where one can get his ducks plucked. Saturday night in Butte City, ducks unlimited.

If I had a town, I would have streets called Easy and Sesame, of course, Right Way, Wrong Way, Positive Way, Drunk Drive, Don't Drive, Can't Drive, My Place, Your Place, Peyton Place, Lois Lane, Left Lane, Memory Lane, Not Taken Road, and Pleasure Path. I would have a road called "The" so people could say they were on the road again. Maybe I'd throw in the alphabet, but I wouldn't put it in sequence, maybe I'd just put in the vowels. The road into my town would be Heavenly Highway, and to get out you'd have to take the Highway to Hell.

Of course, there would have to be intersections that cause you to wonder...like what restaurants are at the corner of Soup and Salad, how many accidents occur at Hit and Run? What happens at the intersection of Rights & Responsibilities? Probably the same stuff that happens at the corner of Common and Sense.

While I'm driving these points home, let's call a gas station a gas station, not a service station, because we forfeit services when we pump our own gas and wash our own windows.

Billboard Heaven

Along Highway 99, there is a billboard advertisement for a mortuary. Not just any mortuary, but a cost-effective mortuary. Like you were driving through Gridley wondering who to call about dead Aunt Clara? Like she's in the backseat, waiting for you to find an affordable funeral home, and doggone if you can think of one. If only there was a sign along the highway, directing you to an inexpensive yet tasteful undertaking. What luck! Here's a happy sign, letting you and Aunt Clara travel worry-free along 99.

Maybe it would make more sense if it were closer to the part of 99 nicknamed "Blood Alley." This is where many motorists have bought tickets to the afterlife. Shouldn't advertisers go where the market exists? There is no Blood Alley billboard, just Gridley, and who dies in Gridley?

I salute the advertisers who make money from the companies they solicit for billboard advertising. Imagine the pitch..."Jim, I can get you a huge sign on I-5, backlit and intense paint. Even drivers going the other way will pull over and look at the sign in awe, and no one on the freeway will be unaware of where to make their next casket purchase."

I'm so sorry if this offends, but do we really think billboards are the correct advertising venue for morticians? I don't know. When family members croak, am I going to go riding around looking to billboards for help?

Another message along 99, a good place to read, was a pro-life public service announcement. It had a photo of a baby and a sonogram, and it read, "They called her fetus, we named her Sydney." When you drive by this really fast, the only thing you think is, "Well, that's a better name."

Recently, there was one of those messages from God on a billboard near a school. It read, "You know that Love Thy Neighbor thing? I meant that." People got incensed. How dare they have a message from God near a school! You could put the pro-life message near the school, but keep the Lord out. Right? How about a great slogan about affordable funerals next to the high school? Would anyone oppose that? How about next to a nursing home?

While it is totally appropriate to advertise food products on billboards, I resent being asked if I have milk. No, not if I have milk, but if I got milk. Wrong sentence structure, bad grammar, sour milk.

Who wants to know what groceries I buy? I think it's pretty suspicious for a billboard to want to know what is in my refrigerator. Is it a plot? I don't think I want to let anyone know if I got milk.

What's next? "Got enough Preparation H for the weekend?" "Got your finger up your nose while you're driving?" Somebody is taking this information seriously. Wait and see.

Don't get me wrong. I am against drunk driving. It is an abomination. However, what is the market for the billboards against drunk driving? Would it be drunk drivers? How could they read them if they're drunk? Would it be potential drunk drivers? "Uhh, I was going to drive drunk, but the sign said not to." It COULD happen.

Would the message be for sober drivers? Why? So again, where's the market? What it really is, folks, is a feel-good campaign. If a drunk driver kills someone, the advertiser and sponsors can say, "We did our part." And the general public can say, "Well, there was a warning sign. Didn't they see it?" And the government can say, "We need more and tougher laws, because the people obviously aren't paying attention to the messages."

If we must see public service announcements on the road, I would like a billboard message or two that reminds people that they are responsible for their own actions. Just that. "You are responsible for your own actions." Nothing from God, Mary, or the Milk Board. Just a notice from every mother's mouth at one time or another...to interpret as you wish.

More Driving Offenses

Let's check your driving record again. It isn't a pretty picture. I'd remind you to go to the DMV and pick up a handbook, but that would mean you'd have to drive down Humboldt Street, where there are other cars coming toward you and the DMV has moved, so there are many variables that could account for your inattention to the wheel. For instance, it could be afternoon.

Humboldt Street is tricky, because there is a center turn lane, and several interesting businesses on either side. Some of you may not have acquainted yourselves with the turn lane. It is the wide space in the middle of the road, outlined in yellow, with arrows pointed in the direction of the businesses. The turn lane is sometimes used for turning. Quite often, though, it is where one drives if the blinkers come on. The drivers of these signaling vehicles often turn the opposite direction of the one indicated. Incidentally, when one is done turning, it is perfectly acceptable to turn off the blinker. In fact, this is preferable. However, you may want to turn again within the hour, so keep it on, don't worry.

This holiday season, I urge you to not only buy your handguns at Wal-Mart, but also some Gingko Biloba, a vitamin that helps you use your brain. Chew them up right in the parking lot, because you're going to need them for the drive home.

Perhaps we should use reverse psychology here. Ok, I know its difficult, but think twice about buckling up. If you don't buckle up, you can get out of the car faster, perhaps through the windshield. However, if you do use your seatbelt, you may not be able to reach the radio dial. You have to have priorities.

Oh, gosh! Are we getting sarcastic here? Well, stop being so sloppy and forgetful on the road.

"Daddy, what do the yellow lines on the road mean?" "That's an imaginary line, little girl. If we drive over it, it means we have a first down, and we are that much closer to getting a touchdown."

"Oh. Daddy, what does that big red sign with the word STOP mean?" "Well, little girl, it has several different interpretations, but basically it means jam out into traffic before anybody else."

"Oh. Daddy, what if I want to stop while I'm driving, just to remember where I'm going?" "Go right ahead and stop in the middle of the road. If you hear someone honking at you, they're just jealous."

"Is there some kind of rulebook where I can learn these things, Daddy?" "Nope, sorry. You're going to have to learn by my example, just like your brother, God rest his soul."

There have been about 10 accidents in the span of two weeks, where CHP officers have written, 'the driver overcorrected and lost control of the vehicle.' This is meant to be a life lesson, but it appears no one is picking it up.

Someday in the future, we'll put driver's training back in school, maybe? Someday when our eyes have grown dimmer, we'll obtain the Driver's Handbook from the DMV and have our children read it to us. And when they come to an exciting part about common sense or using one's judgment, we will listen, ever rapt, and say "What a great book! I wish they had something like that when I was young. Would that I had known to turn from a turn lane. Wow."

We'll have conversations with our children, "Hey, remember when I used to double-park in the no-parking zone across from your school and tell you to run between cars to get to school? I just read in this book that I was doing it all wrong. Boy, it's a wonder you never got run over by the short bus."

Whatever it is that is making you ignore the rules, I hope it is just a phase. (You know how those 38-year-olds are.)

One more thing. When you're parking, those two white lines are supposed to be on each side of the car. It is kind of a guideline to show you where a car ought to fit. If you park directly on one of those lines, you are taking up two spaces, and it's quite possible another person looking for a parking space could get medieval on your "trunk."

Remember the Romper Room lady's advice: Drive with your thinking cap on.

Twisted Survival

Tales of my vacations could likely fill a good comic book. I had that horrible accident two years ago near Reno, and I've been a nervous wreck driving around big rigs ever since. So it follows that I should take a long road trip to Texas and back, right?

On the way to Texas, my best friend Mick and I decided to take a long, leisurely drive and go through a couple states we hadn't experienced before. For him, it was Kansas and Oklahoma. For me, it was Extreme Fear and Dread.

First, we were under the wrong impression of the season. It is not summer. It is Road Construction season. Everywhere we went, there were treacherous one-lane detours and delays and warnings. We became numb to it after Nevada. I should not drive in Nevada. After the accident two years ago, I left myself open for whammies.

Anyway, there is a small town in Nevada called Eureka, where you are cautioned to slow down to 25 miles per hour, so you don't miss it.

Well, I had just slowed down and was moving toward the center of town, when BAM, a deer jumped out of nowhere and hit the passenger side of the car and bounced off. I freaked out. The deer was fine and even looked at me to see if I was all right. Then it took off with some deer friends into the night. The car sustained a small dent. I had a small heart attack, but continued to drive. After the town passed from view, there was a deer warning sign. No wonder I hit the deer – it was out of place.

Next came the mountain. First there was an arrow that indicated the road would have some hairpin turns. Ok, we expected that. So I'm taking these turns at 30 and 35 miles per hour and a semi with three trailers passes me.

Then there is another sign. It says Uneven Road.

After 200 yards, there is another sign, Loose Gravel.

These signs indicate that one should take things easy and go slow on the uneven gravelly twisty road. I did. Other drivers did not like my attitude, but I didn't care. I would go five miles per hour if I had to.

At the summit, there was a sign indicating Fresh Oil on the loose gravel over the uneven twisty road. Mick asked me if I was okay. I said sure, but my grip on the steering wheel was intense. The next sign said No Shoulder. So I'm going 25 mph up a squiggly uneven gravelly road covered with fresh oil, and big rigs are passing me. Then there was another sign to watch for deer. Well, I'd already hit one, I was immune.

A rabbit skitted across the oily, gravelly twisted road onto the non-shoulder, right in front of me. I turned to Mick and said, "He didn't have a sign." But luckily we were coming up on another caution sign, indicating dangerous crosswinds. I lost it. I yelled out the window, "What's next, ICEBERG?" Mick laughed all the way into Utah.

We drove and drove, through Utah, Colorado, Kansas and Oklahoma, heading toward east Texas. At the Oklahoma/Texas boarder, we stopped at a restaurant where a young man asked us, "Y'all want some ice cream t' folla yore meal t'night?" I told him he had a great accent. He said, "Y'all ain't from around here, is ya?"

I told Mick, "We're in the south now." He said, "Boy, let me tell you what. We shore are."

The south has grown. Especially Dallas. It is huge. I'm talking freeway traffic that would scare the Andretti family. Luckily, we found the right road and drove into Frankston, Texas just 48 hours after we left California.

A friend of the family met us at the car and said to me, "I knewed it was you or your sister. Y'all favor."

We spent a few days listening and trying to interpret the drawls, eating fresh catfish and drinking the house wine of the south, iced tea with lots of sugar, and then we decided to head home another way. Route 66.

We also took a side journey to the spectacular Grand Canyon. I looked and looked but could not find the commemorative T-shirt which reads, "I hiked all the way" and in really small letters, "from the car to the guard rail."

From Arizona, we turned north and went through Las Vegas and up through Nevada again, but I guess the deer had warned the others that I might be back. No other wildlife bothered us.

Back home once again, we spent a few hours talking with family members, giving them the highlights of the trip, laughing and making it sound like it was hilarious, but it was the laughter of mentally deranged and exhausted Bambi-bashing Route 66 survivors. It's good to be home.

Chapter 23
TWISTED FAT THOUGHTS

Fat, fat the water rat. Fat as a pig. Fat cow. My fat fanny. Fat as a house. Have another Twinkie. Big-boned. Miss a meal? Here it is, behind you. Fat Albert. Retaining water. Pudgy. Chubby. Extra large. Jumbo. Fatty Arbuckle. Huge. Enormous elephant. Biggie. Fatman and Ribbon. Is it me, or did it just get fatter in here? Between a rock and a fat place. Fat-a-rama. Baby fat. Low fat, no fat, high fat. Big and tall. Short and fat. Here comes the bride, big fat and wide.

I am so sick of being fat. I need to be thin by 5 o'clock. I'm so fat, I look like I ate my inner child. Where did my neck go? Nobody knows the fatness I've seen. Only Sally Struthers could understand.

At birth I weighed 8 pounds and 10 ounces. At age 12, I tipped the scales at 140 pounds. I refuse to disclose the latest tonnage information, but my doctor's office just bought a brand new scale.

My son is 5 foot 10, and weighs 115 pounds. He's a stick, and so is his wife. She is six months pregnant, and hasn't topped 120 pounds. I want to slap her. I am so tired of all these skinny people whining about how fat they are. Puh-leaze!

THE VANILLA PEOPLE

Here's a clue. If spandex hangs on you like it does on the hanger, you are thin. If, however, the threads are poppin' when you pull it over your thigh, you may have a weight problem. You may also have no fashion sense, as spandex was not made to flatter big figures.

I am fat because all my memories revolve around food and the conquest thereof. All the pictures in Mom's photo albums are of people stuffing their faces. All events are planned around the food we will consume, not where we plan to go or what place we might visit, unless you count Denny's. An 80th birthday party just screams lasagna. An anniversary? That will be a huge buffet dinner with a vat of vanilla ice cream for dessert. If someone in the family gets married, the first question is not "Who is the lucky girl/guy?" but "Who will you get to make the cake?"

My son can suck in his stomach to his backbone, making him look like an Ethiopian on a diet. I measured once, and with it sucked in like that, he was a half inch thick from belly button to spine. It's gross and fascinating and you're glad its not you, but you wish you could do it but oh, my God it is so disgusting. Its one of those things you have to look at while you drive by, like a gruesome car accident or a day care center on fire.

He goes to the grocery store with his pregnant wife. They stand behind the cart. They both fit behind the cart without sticking out on either side. They take up two square tiles. My boyfriend and I need two carts, in two separate stores.

I take my son to breakfast. We order omelets and coffee. He gets full on the coffee. Full. Cannot contain more. There's something wrong with him. I don't get full for two more meals and a late night snack.

It's easy to get fat. I've done it for years. Here's how: Eat deep-fat fried mozzarella sticks. Dip them in melted butter. Accompany that cholesterol festival with a double fudge chocolate malted topped with whipped cream. Then eat a whole bag of marshmallows, dipped in caramel. Do this for three meals a day for 21 days. It's that easy. Why isn't there a diet plan that easy?

Why is sudden weight loss so bad for people? All the experts say it is bad, but they never say why. They just say "take off pounds slowly and sensibly." I want it gone now. They make instant pudding, why not instant pudding remover? And for Pete's sake, why do I have to exercise daily to lose weight? I can't jump or bend or breathe while running in place. I'm too fat. I could do it if I was skinny. It doesn't make sense to do it now. And drink eight glasses of water per day? 64 ounces of H2O? That makes me water-logged as well as fat. Love that Titanic feeling.

I hate Richard Simmons and Kathy Smith and Jane Fonda and Susan Powter and that perky little Mary Lou Retton. If I were to lose three or four hundred pounds, I would not want to gain the perky attitude of those folks.

I don't want to be accepted for who I am, either. I want to be accepted as the incredibly thin person I should be after sticking to my diet for a month. On the inside, I am Wonder Woman. The outside should reflect this regardless of whether I faint on the Stairmaster.

Coming Out Fat

After all these years, I must acknowledge the facts and let the world know...I'm fat. There. It is not easy to come out of the closet with this kind of news, especially at my size. But it's time to let the rest of the world know what I've held back for so long. I'm FAT, and I'm coming out of the closet, with bigger clothes.

I've always known I was fat, even as a young girl. Back then, there were different names for my "type," such as "chubby" or "husky." Sometimes I was referred to as a "big" girl, but I knew what those words meant, and I fit the picture. I was born this way.

People act like they don't know what you're talking about when you tell them you're fat. Like they can't tell, unless you're applying for a job. There are ways to tell when there is a fat person in the room. 1) There is less air. 2) All the chocolate pretzels are gone.

But polite people deny fatness. It isn't there, so it isn't a problem.

I recently told my parents I was fat. It was a heartbreaking scene. It was difficult, but I finally got the nerve to say, "Mom, Dad, I have something to tell you…I'm fat." Mom hung her head and cried. She just sobbed and boo-hooed into a dishtowel while Dad fumed and said, "No daughter of mine is fat. Now you just say it isn't so. You are NOT fat, young lady." Mom looked up. "You certainly don't blame us for this, do you?"

I told them there was no blame. "I made the choices, the decisions, its all on me, and it's ok." I had dropped mine, so I didn't need to carry their denial anymore. I told them, "My guilt over enchiladas is really secondary in my life now. I have more important things to bring to therapy."

I did understand their concern for me; after all, there is a lot of prejudice out there against fat people. Oh yeah, even today, in the age of enlightenment. Some people think the fatter you are, the longer it will take for you to get to heaven. Some people think it's a sin to be fat, and fat people shouldn't be allowed to get married or have children. I've heard that some people don't want a fat person to teach their children in school. It might rub off. God, if it would rub off, no one would be fat.

They think if I'm fat I must also be lazy, and I might tell others it is as fun as a carnival to be considered "huge." If I could use my influence to encourage others to be fat, I would be as dumb as some thin folks think I am.

Some fat people fight who they are and some have given up. Most deny it altogether, or at least deny it for someone else. At the doctor's office, when a fat person steps on the scale, whether the weight is up or down, the nurse almost always says, "Well, I never would have believed that."

Some teenage girls say they are fat, just to get attention. They just want someone else to say, "No, you're not. You're a rail." If they really are fat though, nobody pays any attention until it is medically necessary.

Industry caters to thin people, or those trying to be thinner.

Because the economic trend favors the skinny, so does society. This makes it ok for sales clerks to be snooty to people bigger than size 10, and for wedding dresses for "big" girls to be absolutely hideous. It's why we don't surf or ride horseback. It's why we drive small cars.

They say the reason people come out of the closet is because a bell goes off in their head and suddenly there is clarity, and a willingness to share themselves. This is exactly what happened to me. True Story!

I was driving to Krispy Kreme, and I was thinking my snide little sarcastic thoughts, "Uh Oh, they better turn on the fat lady alarm...Fat Lady, now in the Krispy Kreme parking lot...Large woman about to purchase donuts...Whoop Whoop Whoop, etc." And I got out of the car, went into the donut shop expecting the wave of sugar heaven to hit me, and all of a sudden the fire alarm went off, just as I walked in. (There was no fire. A little kid had pulled the alarm to see what would happen.) I thought..."Oh my God. The fat lady alarm...it's real."

So then I knew for sure I was fat, and I have been forthright about it ever since, telling people, "Hi, I'm fat.," just like that guy in the commercial running around annoying people saying he lowered his cholesterol.

It may be annoying, but I say go ahead and sing the body electric. Celebrate the you that's inside and out. Open the closet door(s) and come out fat, like me.

Fat Prejudice

It is ok to be fat, did you know that? I came out of the closet with nothing to wear, and declared to my children, "I AM FAT." This was not news to them, so they continued to watch cartoons.

Actually, I have fat days and thin days. A big fat day is when you wake up and look in the mirror and it appears that your face is a foot wider, your neck has a new ripple, your arms shake when you stop walking, your stomach resembles that of a snake that swallowed a large mammal, your hips touch each wall and your thighs create thunder. You walk by a crowd and hear "Boom, ba ba boom, ba ba boom." The cement cracks. Oh yes, this is a fat day.

I feel fattest when I see thin people wearing the same color as me. Some women look sexy in purple. I look like Barney.

A thin day is when I have 45 cents and two days left until payday, and I'm desperate for a taco. When I actually walk further than a block, and when I drink two bottles of water in a day, I feel extremely thin. Then I reward myself with lasagna.

I am great and powerful and mighty fat when skinny little boys make fun of me. I see myself stepping on them. Squish. Crunch. Flick.

When I visit an ice cream or donut store, I feel all eyes in the parking lot are on me. Caution! Fat lady going in. Make way!"

The words to describe fat are harsh to the ear. Say them in the mirror. FAT, LARD, OBESE, COW, OMNIVORE, HUGE, STOUT, PORTLY, CORPULENT, ROTUND. Each word produces a sour face.

Now say thin words in the mirror. SLIM, THIN, GAUNT, SKINNY, SLIGHT, SLENDER, BONY, LEAN, LANKY, ANOREXIC. It isn't the same effect, is it?

Unfortunately, society thinks slim people are also smarter, whereas fat people are obviously out of control so they must be stupid. This is called PREJUDICE, and it is uglier than a 300 pound woman in zebra striped spandex.

You can smell fat prejudice in the mall. When dresses for big women are called shifts or mu-mus, and dresses for thin women are called sundresses, that's mean. When a big woman goes into a store near the thin clothes, the clerks either hide or get snotty. When there is a "Plus-Size" department, all the dresses look like boxes – they're designed by thin people with a mean streak. There's a neck hole and two arm holes, but otherwise, they could be Hefty bags. The next time some clerk wants me to announce what size I wear, I'm going to say "33-gallon."

Thin people better stop thinking I'm stupid. I'm not. I've just never met a donut I didn't like. I've also met plenty of thin people who are definitely out of control.

Here are my fat excuses. I've had two children and never lost the weight I gained when pregnant. (Or the shape.) Granted, it has been 25 years. How about this? I was raised on buttermilk and corn. No? How about – Dimples show up better on chubby cheeks. Or, fat little redheads sell the most Girl Scout cookies. My favorite excuse is, "I had planned on being thin, but then Satan told me to pick up that Twinkie."

I don't care for a traditional diet. My favorite foods are not necessarily unhealthy. I could live on spinach, pepper jack cheese and root beer, with the occasional dessert of tapioca pudding. Would that be horrible?

The problem is that all diets call for increasing one's water intake. I don't like water. Water bites. I only like water that comes through the coffee pot and turns dark brown.

Traditional diets also call for increased exercise. I'm too tired. Sometimes I'm too tired to type the word exercise, much less do sit-ups. I'm also too fat to exercise. Only thin people should bend over. That makes sense, doesn't it?

You call a tall person when you want something off the top shelf. You should call a thin person when you drop your pencil.

I think it shouldn't matter if you have a butt like a credenza or thighs that stretch across county lines. No one should look down on you for eating a candy bar or six.

Santa Claus is fat and everyone loves him. They even leave fattening food out for him. The tooth fairy is thin, and all she gets for it is used teeth, and she has to pay for them.

It's more fun to hug a fat person than a thin one. And I'd rather sit on Santa's lap than some skinny guy's bony knees. Fat people know comfort. They know pleasure. They don't torture themselves running around a track.

I am having a very FAT day.

White Woman Explodes

I have no doubt how I'm going to die some day. I am going to walk out in the sun and pop. The above headline will likely be one of the bizarre titles in the Enquirer when I go.

I am definitely a winter person. Summer makes me want to run and hide. I have said before that I have Irish white flammable skin, but I have never alluded to the dangers of this condition.

I cannot go outside without getting burned, despite being covered in "50" sun block. My skin is so white, others have to wear shades to avoid the blinding glare. Now you know why I don't wear shorts. I am protecting you.

I am close to what you could call translucent. The sun sees me and starts thinking "Hmm. Time to fry a couch potato." I get freckles just by looking out the window.

Once when I was 8, I had a new swimsuit and my sister rubbed baby oil on my back just prior to our visit to Santa Cruz beach. In fact, I was only exposed to the sun from the time we walked two blocks from the car to the beach, stepped foot in the ocean and decided it was too cold. That was maybe 15 minutes.

The rest of the day I sat in the shade of an umbrella with zinc on my nose. When we got home, my back and legs were covered with blisters and I was a lobster red that you know would never "turn into a tan."

I not only bake, but I melt. So it makes sense I live in the Sacramento Valley, right? I find Popsicles absolutely necessary for survival.

My friends have called me page-white, because I'm a writer. I said, "Ha. Cute." I've also been called sheet-white, ghost white and GE the 40 watt light bulb. I hate going to the beach because of my resemblance to Casper.

I've always wanted to be a six-foot tall blonde with a deep brown tan, like a Susan Anton or Bridgette Nielsen or Bo Derek. Imagine how it feels to strive for Loni Anderson and hit Jerry Stiller.

I yearn for the day that sexy means a short, plump redhead with creamy skin. Oh, yeah babe. Unfortunately, I find discrimination in this area. People are prejudiced against folks with extremely white skin. Especially folks with too much white skin.

When I go shopping with my daughter, we've been in stores for small, tanned girls, and the sales clerks have been especially snobby to me. Not the regular snobbiness of those who must work in retail, but a coolness more often associated with a Mercedes dealer encountering a bag lady. How dare I breathe on their skinny clothes meant to show off browned legs?

I don't deal well with these bigots. If they come up to me with their noses up, asking "Can I help you pick something out for a friend?" I tell them I don't know anyone with bulimia. Then I might scratch myself inappropriately. If I got really mad, I might show them my legs and blind them.

The Perfect Time to Diet

I don't want to exercise. I want the fat to melt off really fast, like when you put a Junior Mint on the sidewalk in July.

They all tell me, "It doesn't work that way." I say, well, why not? Why hasn't someone invented a way we can all become Twiggy? (For those of you with no sense of history before 2000, Twiggy was a model before they called them supermodels, and she was the epitome of "thin.")

Every year just prior to swim suit season, some major poll comes out with the percentage of Americans who are obese, and its usually like 80 to 90 percent (mostly women over 35 with red hair.) This poll discourages the mass purchase of bathing suits and simultaneously increases the sales of a variety of diet and exercise items. At the same time, the ice cream industry comes out with new flavors for those who have no hope.

The "get thin" industry is huge, and needs to go on a diet. They try to make us think that being six feet tall and weighing 80 pounds would be ideal. You know, give me a size 4 or give me death.

There is really no good time to diet and exercise. In January, you are recovering from the past year's holiday season and eating heartily because it is winter.

In February, any plans to diet are ruined by Valentines Day, whether your love buys you a box of chocolate or you buy your own because you have no sweetheart. In March, you have plans to run, but it rains. Then you drink too much green beer on St. Patrick's Day so you don't recover until April, and then there's your Easter basket full of malted milk balls and marshmallow peeps.

In May, you start having barbecues and tons of potato salad. In June, July and August, who doesn't beat the heat with ice cream? September brings Monday Night Football with the obligatory parties that include beer and hot wings and potato chips and more beer.

October is no time to diet, because you have to buy Halloween candy, and then you have to buy more Halloween candy before Halloween because you ate the first bag. How can anyone diet in November with Thanksgiving coming up? And in December, there are all those Christmas parties.

So you tell me when its possible to diet. And if I'm not dieting, why exercise? A person doesn't take off any fat by doing jumping jacks without foregoing s'mores. Plus there are no good ways to exercise without having a stroke.

Running sucks. Richard Simmons tapes? Forget it. Line-dancing? Aaaauuuggghhh! Going to a gym, you are sure to be surrounded by big-haired, leopard print leotard wearing heroin thin girls and half-brained muscle bound jocks trying to pick them up. Sound like fun to you?

Stairmasters are evil. Who needs them? If you could choose where you're going to die of a heart attack, would it be on a Stairmaster surrounded by skinny, sweaty people in spandex or at a corner table in a restaurant surrounded by your loving family, enjoying wine and red meat?

Having cursed the diet and exercise game, I'm actually drinking the water and taking a yoga class. I have forced myself against my will to stretch and bend and go to the bathroom 90 times a day. Curse Jane Fonda. I can do this. I have raised two teenagers.

I am fond of yoga, because as a child I would watch the Yoga woman on TV and imitate her and I did very well. Once my sister watched with me and got stuck in the lotus position. I helped her free herself, because it was her turn to do the dishes.

I think yoga might be good for me. Twisted mind, twisted body.

Middle Name—Grace

I have the soul of a dancer. Unfortunately, I have the body of a large sea-going mammal. I remember taking ballet lessons, and tap dancing, and something called "modern movement" which was introduced in the 70's as an interpretive dance class that included jazz-aerobics, pantomime, Greco-roman wrestling and jumping about with a long piece of see-through material, trying not to trip over it.

I have always been a writer, but at age six, I thought I'd have a sideline as a ballerina. I remember all the positions and the terminology. I can still stand on my toes and I can even do the splits, because despite my whining about exercise, I am pretty limber for a fat girl.

I can dance. I can do the twist. I waltz and reggae, I can tap, do a grand jete, and finish with the Hustle. I can even belly dance, but I have too much belly.

They say fat people shouldn't dance. Hey, they are wrong. Some of us charm the shoes off the folks on the dance floor. There are plenty of thin people who can only do the opposable thumb dance, leaning from side to side and sticking out their thumbs as if hitch hiking to the next dance floor. It isn't pretty. Some rather buoyant people actually have rhythm. And women, God bless us, do it backward and in high heels.

Oddly enough, this is not a challenge to me, because I have that soul of a dancer thing going, and if I fall over, I'm taking someone else with me, so we can both laugh. I dance everywhere, even in my car. My kids hate to go to the grocery store with me because I will start rocking out to the Muzak. "Mom, you promised you wouldn't do the Macarena in the Produce section anymore!" I tell them to shut up or I'll sing, too.

In modern dance, I learned to be "interpretive." To me, it meant "act like you're full of emotion." I tried. It was in my soul, but it had a hard time getting to my feet. I found out I would be a better comedian than ballerina. But it was ok, because of that soul thing.

Men often "interpret" dance badly, especially white men who lived through the disco era without getting a date. They made up their own rules on the dance floor. They thought, "If I shift from one foot to the other about 75 times, I can call that dancing. If I include slight arm movement or snapping fingers, I am a GOOD dancer. If I flap my arms like a giant bird and hop from one foot to the other in a box pattern, people will not notice my socks don't match. And if I copy a few Travolta moves or let out a loud whoop in the middle of a song, my partner will end up cooking me breakfast."

They were mistaken.

My ex-husband used to leave me on the dance floor whenever he disagreed with the lyrics. He did not want to go to Funkytown.

By then, I was used to humiliation. I never went to my senior prom. I stayed home and wrote mean things about the prom queen, Carmie. She didn't dance well, but she grew up blonde and beautiful, despite being in the same accordion class as me in second grade. Fate should have worked the same for her as for me, based on accordion lessons, don't you think? But no, I'm the one who dances in the canned fruit aisle. I'm sure Carmie goes to a more expensive store and dances near the imported food. She probably does that thumb dance in front of the tofu.

Nightmare on Plumas Street

I had the fat dream again. Do you know the one I mean? It is so like a horror movie.

Fade in. I'm sitting at my dining room table, my normal fat self, and before me is a plate full of Twinkies. I reach for one, naturally. As I touch it, my arm gains 25 jiggling pounds.

I bring the tasty golden morsel to my lips and take a bite. I suddenly weigh more than a thousand pounds and my chair gives. I hardly notice. I reach for another Twinkie, and instantly put on another ton. The carpet is ripped and the floor cracks, up to the front door.

I pick up the plate of Twinkies and toss them all into the cavern that has become my mouth. I am suddenly outside, probably because I no longer fit in any building.

I'm thinking, "Wow, I'm taller." But I pay no attention to the tremendous impact my tonnage is having on the environment. I am cracking the streets with each step. I've killed several neighborhood cats and flattened a few cars, as my footsteps determine the destiny of others.

All this time I have not regretted a moment of fatness, only reveled in my power. I have become the FAT Monster. My laugh is evil and it echoes through the streets of Willows. "Give me your Twinkies," I shout.

I pick up the Hostess truck and empty its contents into my mouth. Then I throw the truck like a Tonka. It lands on a couple of skinny people walking a few streets away. I jump for joy, causing an earthquake.

"Coffee!" I yell, looking around for a drink. The people have erected a giant cup by this time, and are pouring hundreds of gallons of delicious caffeine and hazelnut creamer into it. I take the roof off of Holiday market and reach in for some Sweet & Low. All the Sweet & Low.

Some guy is still pouring coffee into the cup when I grab it and bring it up to my mouth. He falls off the handle and screams all the way down to the sidewalk. I laugh and squash him like a bug. He looked like my ex-husband.

After drinking my coffee, I take a walk. Its only a couple of steps to Sacramento and then I turn left and walk over the pass and go to

Reno, growing tremendously with each step. I'm thinking these were extra special Twinkies.

I stomp on people and cars all over Interstate 80, and I look magnificent, my hair blowing in the wind, my rolls of fat whipping back and forth, causing sonic booms. It isn't like the Incredible Hulk, because my clothes still fit. Never underestimate the power of stretch pants. My shoes grow with my feet, too. There's something special about PF Flyers.

At the beginning of this whole dream, the theme of the Wicked Witch of the West is playing. Then it's Don Henley singing "All She Wants To Do Is Dance."

I stomp all over Nevada and Arizona. Suddenly, my foot gets caught in the Grand Canyon. I'm stuck. I can't move. I holler for more Twinkies and coffee, but my voice is too loud to understand. Here's where it gets weird.

All these horses and men with ropes are trying to free my foot from the canyon. They are working so hard they turn purple. I pick them up and they are grapes. I eat them. Fresh fruit is important in a well-balanced diet.

Finally I grow out of the canyon, and keep walking eastward, stomping everything in my path. After I mess up the south and the east, I head north and wash my hands in the Great Lakes. I stomp and stomp all over America. I am so big now my head is in the ozone. I don't see any holes.

I walk back across the top of the US, where the dotted line is, and pick up a few grizzly bears in Alaska to see if I like bear meat. It's yummy. I step over to Willows to get my cup, and I go east again, to drink whatever chocolate is left at the Hershey plant. I have destroyed most of the country when I hear a small voice. It is my conscience.

It says "Your butt is 6000 miles wide, but its smaller than your stomach." I have heard my conscience say this many times before, but now it is actually true.

I reach across the ocean and pick up the Eiffel Tower. I slowly finger the sharp point, then close my eyes and stab my stomach. As I pop like a balloon, all this wind covers the earth, restoring America while I shrink at an incredible rate.

Suddenly, I'm back in California, sitting at my table with the Twinkies. I start to reach for one. I go through the whole dream again and again.

The third and fourth time I reach for that first Twinkie, I hear thousands of people screaming. Finally, when I pop myself for the fourth time with the Eiffel Tower, I hear a buzzing sound and I wake up to my alarm.

Hmm. Breakfast time. For some reason I want French toast. Then on the way to work, I passed a Hostess truck, and I smiled like Mona Lisa and waved at the driver.

The Road to Fatness is Paved with Sugar

People who write diet books and scare pamphlets for your doctors office often put in "ideal" 7- or 21-day diet plans that include melba toast. These plans are almost always written by people who could never pinch an inch. I could write a "How to Get Extremely Fat and Worry Your Doctor" plan, but people don't seem to want to hear it, even though my plan would include a lot of chocolate and whipped cream and not one bite of melba toast.

Who eats Melba toast anyway? You might as well eat the box it came in. Yummy. Its about as exciting as a bran muffin.

Here is a sample day on the healthy plan, and my fat plan on the right.

Breakfast:	Breakfast:
1 cup grapefruit juice	3 cups coffee (with Sweet & Low &
1 cup cooked oatmeal	flavored creamer) 1 more cup after
½ cup skim milk	you get dressed.
Sprinkle wheat germ	1 cup ice cream or whatever is left

THE VANILLA PEOPLE

Lunch:
Fruit salad plate w/ 1 ½
Cups sliced mixed fresh
Fruit, with ½ cup low-
fat yogurt
4 slices melba toast
1 iced tea w/lemon

Dinner:
½ skinless chicken breast
baked with thyme and
rosemary; ½ cup rice
½ cup steamed asparagus
iced tea with lemon
1 small biscuit (2 inch square)
with 1 tsp soft margarine
1 cup grapes

Snack
4 graham crackers
1 cup skim milk

Snack:
3 cookies
1 more cup coffee w/
additives

Lunch:
Double cheeseburger &
fries
40 ounce soda

Snack:
Fruit salad plate w/ 1 ½ cups
sliced mixed fresh fruit and
container of yogurt; 4 slices
toast
1 slice chocolate cream pie

Dinner:
2 Barbecued pork chops, drip
ping w/ southern bbq sauce;
mashed potatoes and thick
gravy; carrots in raspberry
sauce

2 glasses Chardonnay
1 cup coffee

Snack:
3 slices of sourdough French
bread, w/ melted garlic
cheddar cheese; rest of the
wine.

   My diet plan is Killer, ain't it?
   I'm on the sugar highway to a heart attack or stroke, which really bites, because the road to health doesn't have a fast food restaurant

in sight. My doctor says its "dyslipidemia" which means "You're fat." My cholesterol and blood pressure numbers are bad. I said, "Well, change the numbers."

She didn't get it. She said, "You have to change those numbers through diet (we hear a scream) and exercise. (another scream)" And pills. So I pop pills like it was the '60's. But I refuse the 2 ounces of high protein non fat salt free triglyceride lowering unsweetened skim nonhydrogenated diet food in the heart attack warning pamphlet. And my yoga tapes look good sitting next to the TV. And my Abs for Women book has a great binding. We wouldn't want to mess that up.

89 TABS TO GO

I'm sticking to my resolution, regardless that the year is half over. I will be healthier at the end of this year if it kills me. I am alive today, despite having opened my new bottle of vitamins this morning. What follows is an attempt at descriptive visualization of the aromatic olfactory stimuli released upon the occasion of the contravention of the sealed container of the alleged nutritive supplements.......

BLECCCCCHHHH!

Let me put it another way.

Imagine traveling in the back of a poorly operating bus seated behind four or five large, sweaty, unbathed men who all ate heaps of broccoli for lunch and Mexican food for dinner, then played with a mangy dog on a cow pasture next to a landfill. The bus windows are sealed shut with mildew and the lavatory door keeps flying open with every bump and curve, revealing a pair of stiff gym socks, unlaundered for several months, draping the empty soap container. But wait, there's more.

In front of the men, a baby is spitting up and in critical need of a new diaper, next to his mother, who is smiling at you with yellow, tartar-caked teeth, as she bites into a moldy peach. Across the aisle is a hirsute woman whose deodorant quit working several weeks prior to this ride. The bus driver is experiencing a bout of lactose intolerance. Someone's carry-on luggage is emitting a green cloud of salmonella and putrid air from bacteria-laden, week-old raw liver.

The essence of this entire experience is miraculously, succinctly vacuum-sealed within the small bottle of daily multi-vitamin tabs (for women 50 and under) which I began taking today because they are good for me.

Chapter 24
TWISTY HOLIDAYS

What's This Month?

They always warn you too late. There's less than a week left of April and now there's a new ad on the radio about April being Earthquake Preparedness month. Oops. You have four days left to prepare. All of a sudden it will be May and you'll be unprepared. Luckily, May isn't Earthquake Month.

What we need is a list. If each month is dedicated to a cause, and the powers that be know the specific cause for each month, it ought to be easy enough to generate a list of 12. But no, they wait until the 25th of each month to announce what crusade that month should embrace.

People in our office go around the first week of each month asking, "Do you know what last month was?" And we are the media!

We did find out that Breast Cancer Month and Domestic Violence Prevention Month go hand in hand, so to speak. One follows the other, during a gloomy time of year. Hmm.

I am making up my own list because I'm tired of finding out too late. I think each cause should fit the month. Let's base some part of our lives on logic, huh?

January should be Homeless Month. Start at the beginning of the year with coats and warm clothing giveaways, donations to shelters and food banks, and empowering folks to help themselves. Don't put it off like you did your New Year's Resolution.

February is and should be Heart Month. It only makes sense to become more aware of heart disease as you eat a box of chocolates, and give to the American Heart Association, or at least read a story about Barney Clark.

March should be Civil Rights Month. March, civil rights, get it?

April should be Allergy Month. Trust me. Sneezing is at an all time high in April. There should be antihistamine giveaways and people with severe allergies should be given a discount when they buy stock in Kleenex.

May should be Memorial Month. Why just have a few days a year to honor veterans? Take a whole month and do it right. Our military heroes deserve it.

June ought to be Just Say No Month. We need a whole month dedicated to fighting drug and alcohol abuse. Summer is a great time to stop using, since there are so many other things to do. This would be easy to remember, too. June and junkie have the same first three letters.

July should be Vacation Month. Uh oh, there's that logic again. Those who take vacations in July should be given discounts everywhere they go, especially if they travel with their family in a car across more than one state.

August should be Obesity Month. More fat people melt in August than any other summer month. Also, most reports of humans experiencing spontaneous combustion happen in August.

September must be Education Month. Back to school sales are not enough. All schools ought to get extra funding in September. Parents of high school seniors should be warned they will be going into bankruptcy this year.

October should be Old People Month. All senior citizens should be honored; programs that help seniors should get all kinds of funding. This is the only month that commercials should be aired for Depends, and please, not during the dinner hour.

November should be No Smoking Month. No-Vember, they could call it. Here's an incentive. Stop smoking in November and win a prize from all the things left over from the Price is Right that nobody won. It could work.

December ought to be, and in a lot of homes already it is Skip the Bills Month, so we can spend more on Christmas presents for the kids.

However, celebrations or campaigns based on logic may never catch on, since we depend on the GOVERNMENT to tell us what happiness to pursue. I merely offer the above for those who think deeply.

If you write your congressman in favor of the above list, they will put you in a particular file. It may not be pretty. Its probably better to remain uninformed and wonder what month it is.

The Twisted Irish Munchkin

Happy St. Patrick's Day. I have always liked this holiday because green stuff is way cool and because this holiday, more than any other, shaped my future career.

When I was in elementary school, we always had an Irish assembly in the multi-purpose room on or near St. Patrick's Day. We had to sing all the Irish songs and put on a show of St. Patrick the Snake Fighter.

It was from these performances that I grew as a writer. I wrote enthusiastically about our second graders singing "When Irish Eyes Are Smiling" in our school paper, The Greenbrae Herald.

It was actually a class assignment to write about the St. Pat celebration, but my two paragraphs were chosen three years in a row to be the sentiments of the entire student body. I was stoked.

I am of Irish descent, and I can fake the accent pretty well. My family used to amuse themselves by calling me the "leprechaun" due to my lack of height. They loved it when I accused them of stealing my lucky charms.

It used to be that the "wearin' o' the green" was a sacred tradition to avoid getting pinched. Well, one is not allowed to pinch at school anymore, as I found out when my son got suspended.

But back in the old days when I was in third grade, it was an unwritten rule to try to wear a sneaky green, or hidden green, to prove your Irish slyness. One girl I knew fooled everyone with a piece of green yarn braided into her hair. Clever.

My friends and I hunted down those who forgot to wear green, and they'd go home all pinched up and hating March. The bad girls at school would say they had green underwear on, and the boys would chase them to get a look.

In fourth grade, my teacher Mrs. Borgman was the genius. She wore no visible green, but you couldn't pinch her. The soles of her shoes were green as grass.

If you pinched someone who was really wearing green, they got to sock you twice in the arm. You had to be careful who you accused of being non-Irish.

If I ever forgot (as if) to wear green on St. Patrick's Day, they said I was still covered because my eyes are green. Well, that's just cheating. Plain and simple.

Now its not a matter of forgetting. Its clutter. I can't find them, but hopefully I will before its too late – I have green buttons. "Kiss My Blarney Stone" and "No Pinch Zone" and "World's Tallest Leprechaun."

The G rated drink of the day is the Shamrock Shake. Normally I dislike mint ice cream, but I have to have a Shamrock Shake every March or it doesn't feel like a holiday. Last year, McDonalds was a little slow on the uptake. It was March 8, and I ordered a Shamrock Shake, and the counter person said, "We only do that in March." It makes you wonder what the employees smoke. I had to go 30 miles for my Shamrock fix.

Growing up in Reno, I knew something of adult nightlife, and every March it revolved around "green beer." This was what they called it before it had been consumed, which was slightly scary.

On the evening of March 17 in Reno, if you step outside, you can hear Irish songs being sung by many a drunk. It's the melody in the air, accompanied by a green fog.

March is also tornado season, and Hollywood had the foresight to present "The Wizard of Oz" every March on TV. So March, to me, was always this month-long cosmic celebration of short people: leprechauns, munchkins, flattened witches, second-graders and snakes. What's not to love?

Easter Pizza

Some people just try too hard to make everything turn out perfect, and it causes the opposite cosmic effect. For instance, I have tried for many years to have wonderful Easters. So far, only one has managed to be less than disastrous.

Hundreds of years ago when I was very young, on Easter Sunday we had to get dressed up in our pinkest, fluffiest dresses, wearing hats and gloves and carrying small white purses containing two dimes and a Kleenex, and my mother curled our hair severely and took us to church.

There has never been good weather at Easter time in Nevada, even if it was late April. When it is tornado season in Kansas, in Nevada, some of that wind invariably touches down at the Assembly of God Easter Egg Hunt. It was not good to weigh less than 50 pounds in a wind like that. In 1966, more than a dozen little children were blown across the Sierras while hunting for eggs.

There would always be an Easter Egg Hunt planned following the service. Every year, I lost my hat. And most years, I got in fights with the boys after Sunday School, (Girls with freckles, dimples or glasses got teased unmercifully and I had all three afflictions.) and my frilly dresses were shredded and my gloves were dirty from throwing rocks and eggs. I never beaned anyone, though. I had very bad aim. (Let's just say they knew they had to run, because if I caught them, I could deliver pain.)

Most of the time, the egg hunts were cancelled due to blizzard conditions, and the adults didn't want to hide the eggs in the snow. We had modified egg hunts in our living room, and there were at least two years when one of the eggs was found months later. Trust me, that was not pleasant.

Later, with my own children, coloring the eggs was tedious, and half of them turned out grey, because they wanted to mix all the colors together. Also, they caught on early that hunting eggs was not as much fun as hiding them. They would go out in the back yard and find all the ones we hid, and then re-hide them. There are still some missing.

As an adult, I was expected to make an Easter feast. The most disastrous one of all was in 1988. Wanting everything to be perfect, I planned a menu weeks in advance, booked a gazebo at the park, bought comfy folding chairs for the adults and made rabbit ears for each kid. I cooked ham, asparagus, hot rolls, butter beans, deviled eggs, and made a huge fabulous salad. I got matching plates and forks to take to the park, and pastel colored napkins. Everything was going to be wonderful. The day before Easter was a spectacular day, almost summer-like.

We woke up Easter morning to three feet of snow. Remembering prior experience, I denied my children an Easter egg hunt in the living room. Then, just like a biblical movie shown every Easter, thousands of disagreeable family members parted the snow banks and showed up for an Easter feast. They whined about the snow and tromped it into my house, grinding it into the carpet.

Everyone under 12 became involved in a game called "Chase the other kids down the hall." All the adults sat in my living room bitching about the lovely weather. I was left alone in my kitchen putting together Plan B, a spectacular dining room gala. Just as I was about to call everyone into the Martha Stewart dining room, my son let the dog in the back door. In a matter of two seconds, the dog had completely destroyed the kitchen and taken the ham to the corner and was chawing on it hungrily. Everyone walked into the dining room and simultaneously said "Uh-oh."

I don't know what happened after that. I think I blacked out. When I woke up, I was in my bedroom, and my husband had brought in a ham & pineapple pizza to share.

After the divorce, I didn't have to cook, clean or hide eggs. No dresses, hats, gloves or rocks. I let everyone else have their shot at making a feast, and a couple years ago I got to watch the face of my grandson as he found his first grey egg. Now, that was a perfect day.

You know, the closer we get to Easter, pizza doesn't sound half-bad.

Easter Week Conspiracies

The government has messed up Easter for me. They were the ones who came up with the Bunny, and the colored eggs and ham dinner with Grandma. As far as I'm concerned, the only bunny worth talking about is Bugs. And coloring eggs makes my coffee cups smell like vinegar. And believe it or not, our family is trying to stay away from pork.

The biblical story of Easter includes Old and New Testament. Old Testament is the story of Moses, and to help the government, TV networks plan on running "The Ten Commandments" about 15 or 20 times, while advertising that the "Prince of Egypt" is out on video.

When I was little, I thought Charlton Heston was really Moses. Now that he's an advocate for the NRA, I can't make the connection anymore. I can't see Moses with a hand cannon, although negotiations may have been easier when he was arguing with Pharaoh to let his people go. They re-made Romeo and Juliet with guns, why can't they do the same for the Bible?

One Easter Sunday when I lived in Reno, ABC played "The Ten Commandments" in its entirety. It's a fairly long film, right? Well, right after the movie, I hope parents put the kiddies to bed because then the TV played "The Sentinel," a horror movie about the changing of the guardian of the gates of hell, so as not to let all the demons out. It was just the wrong direction to go, after being on Mount Sinai.

The Old Testament is still celebrated today with Passover. Except now they just have a dinner, rather than actually spread lambs blood over the front door, so the angel of death doesn't visit the first-born son. And nowadays, nearly everyone has a back door. Shouldn't the lamb's blood be over every portal? A death angel would be smart enough to come in the bathroom window, I think. Just to be on the safe side, I tell my son to eat a lamb chop and stay inside that day.

The New Testament is revealed with a plethora of movies regarding the life and death and rise from death of Christ. The true message of Easter is lost on the kids, though, because they are not watching the movies. they are thinking about Easter baskets full of candy. You kind of have to re-direct them, to let them know this weekend was about the systematic torture and execution of a man by the government, only this time they chose the wrong man, because he lives.

I don't know how this weekend now seems to be about fuzzy stuffed bunnies from Wal-Mart, but I'm sure it has something to do with taking the focus off of big government.

The day Jesus was nailed to the cross is called Good Friday. That just proves my point that the government is involved. If it were you or me, we would not refer to it as a good day. Fridays are generally good days, because they lead to the weekend, but this one, I think, needs to be renamed. I have colored eggs with my children for more than 20 years. We always have the one last egg that everybody dips in a different color, and it ends up a strange grey shade.

"That one is for Dad," they used to say. Spiral cut glazed ham with either cherry Cumberland sauce or pineapple/clove/brown sugar sauce is just awesome. Now that my daughter is a vegetarian and we've learned that pork is not so good for us anyway, it's harder to enjoy. I didn't say we stopped eating it entirely, just that we have to be less audible in our pork appreciation. No standing ovations.

I hate Easter egg hunts. Hiding them is tough if you have kids who find things easily along with kids who don't. Hunting them is even worse, because the kids who don't find things easily start to give up and whine, while the other kids have 8 or 9 eggs in the first 20 seconds. Also, in 20 years of Easter egg hunts, we probably had 3 that were happily in good weather. All the others were accomplished in rainy, windy, or snowy weather.

The kids didn't mind finding eggs in the snow, but frozen hard boiled eggs don't translate into deviled eggs very well. And there's always that danger of not finding one egg, and finding it 6 months later. "That one is for Dad," they always said. I always thought the best part of Easter was going to church in a new pink dress and hat and gloves. My daughter will be happy to get a new pair of jeans. Things have changed.

Happy Easter!

Rethinking the Calendar

Sometimes you need a new plan for the universe, just to shake things up.

I recently celebrated my half-birthday. There are no age-numbers involved, only cake, ice-cream, and spending money.

I need to celebrate the half-way mark because: A) my actual birthday is Christmas, and no one ever comes over and says Happy Birthday on Christmas; and B) I'm old enough that I may die before my actual birthday happens; and C) What else are you going to do between Flag Day and Fourth of July? Listen, the holidays are all messed up. There are too many in the winter months, and no chocolate-receiving happens during the summer. Critical revision time.

In Sri Lanka, there are 246 holidays per year. That's about 21 per month. Imagine celebrating 21 holidays per month. We'd hardly ever work. How do those Sri Lankians manage to party so much and work so little?

Furthermore, what could they possibly find to celebrate? After 20 or 30 holidays, wouldn't you be sort of less enthusiastic? Wouldn't you start having to celebrate rather benign or insignificant events? What is the next one, Roadkill Day? Smile at Your Next-Door Neighbor Day? How about Septic Tank Celebration Week, the National Cheez-Whiz Salute or Learning to Parallel Park Day? I'm sure there are people who could cater such events and Hallmark has a card for just about everything.

I suggest a change of the American calendar to celebrate 24 legal, paid holidays—that's just two per month less than Sri Lanka, but more than your employer currently offers.

In January, of course, there would have to be New Years Day, and Martin Luther King Day. Let's not change that, but add presents. Gifts are good.

In February, let's go back to Lincoln's birthday and Washington's birthday. Take out Valentine's Day. Don't get upset, we'll move it to another month. And sorry, I don't care to celebrate Groundhog Day. I don't give a damn what rodents think about the weather. In March, let's do St. Patrick's Day on a Friday or a Monday, no matter when the 17th falls, and let'$ add Easter Sunday at the end of the month. Make it a permanent spot on the calendar, rather than jumping back and forth from March to April, don't you agree?

In April, put Mother's Day in the middle, and April Fools Day at the end. I always need extra time to come up with a really good practical joke. For May, put Valentine's Day in the middle, throw in a ham dinner to offset the chocolate, and have Memorial Day at the end of the month, as usual.

In June, let's have Father's Day at the end, and require a new holiday on June 6, to honor World War II veterans. Yes, it is a significant date. Look it up.

In July, there will be Independence Day (do the Friday or Monday thing again) and Hottest Day of the Year National Barbecue Day at the end of the month.

In August, let's have an early Christmas, in the summer heat. Maybe call it

AuggieChristmas. Have that at the beginning of August, and

AuggieChannukah at the end. Have people of all religions celebrate both days.

In September, there will be Labor Day, and Football Season Appreciation Day. Actually, Labor Day could be replaced by Back To School Day. It makes more sense. No one actually works on Labor Day.

In October let's have Oktoberfest at the beginning, and borrow Thanksgiving for the end. Let's do away with Halloween, since it's not safe anymore anyway.

In November, there will be Veterans Day and Grandparent Appreciation Day. Then in December, I suggest another holiday for veterans on Dec. 7. Veterans are true heroes and deserve at least three holidays a year. Think of how many days they served for us.

Then on Dec. 31, the only two-day/two year celebration, New Year's Eve. That should spread it out. Let me sell you on this. The more holidays you give your employees, the less sick time is used, and the higher the morale. Yeah, that's it. Just think of the savings!

The way we've spread it out, you'll spend less at the grocery store, and if relatives come over for AuggieChristmas, they can bring their sleeping bags and tents, and camp out in the front yard. This will likely prevent any family fights. Then people will start to smile more at work and stop going postal, and eventually there will be world peace, all because of MY ittle boys would get firecrackers and hurt themselves setting them off. This would be directly following a safety demonstration by the Fire Department. Later, the city band would play all the patriotic and folksy tunes they could remember, from America the Beautiful to The Streets of Laredo. From God Bless America to I Wish I Was In Dixie. Kids my age (12) would be yelling our requests. ."Do something from Led Zeppelin!!" and "We want Pink Floyd!" We weren't into disco. Just as the sun was setting, there was a parade of veterans, and every citizen was on his feet to applaud our heroes. Vets from Viet Nam, Korea, World War II and World War I would march and bring out the flag, and the applause wouldn't stop. A local school girl would be dressed as Lady Liberty. One year she carried a real torch, and she fell, igniting the grass behind the bleachers. Then there were baton twirlers, the Nevada Rangerettes. They hardly ever dropped a baton. Even the little ones. Of course, they had small batons. Back then, folks were patriots without question. As I entered my teen years, the Viet Nam war became something to fight about, and slowly, heroes began to fade. Folks began to protest, burn bras and flags and draft cards, and wonder what the fighting was all about. Things changed and twisted, and there was a slow burn out. It wasn't popular anymore to be patriotic. It was more popular to snub the militaittle boys would get firecrackers and hurt themselves setting them off. This would be directly following a safety demonstration by the Fire Department.

Later, the city band would play all the patriotic and folksy tunes they could remember, from America the Beautiful to The Streets of Laredo. From God Bless America to I Wish I Was In Dixie. Kids my age (12) would be yelling our requests. ."Do something from Led Zeppelin!!" and "We want Pink Floyd!" We weren't into disco.

Just as the sun was setting, there was a parade of veterans, and every citizen was on his feet to applaud our heroes. Vets from Viet Nam, Korea, World War II and World War I would march and bring out the flag, and the applause wouldn't stop. A local school girl would be dressed as Lady Liberty. One year she carried a real torch, and she fell, igniting the grass behind the bleachers. Then there were baton twirlers, the Nevada Rangerettes. They hardly ever dropped a baton. Even the little ones. Of course, they had small batons.

Back then, folks were patriots without question. As I entered my teen years, the Viet Nam war became something to fight about, and slowly, heroes began to fade. Folks began to protest, burn bras and flags and draft cards, and wonder what the fighting was all about. Things changed and twisted, and there was a slow burn out. It wasn't popular anymore to be patriotic. It was more popular to snub the military and hiss about the government. We forgot about pride. We forgot about what Grandpa did over there. We became complacent about D Day and Pearl, and men shot down over the Sea of Japan, and hundreds of thousands of dead soldiers. What happened to us? We became jaded and arrogant.

Last year, in September, the pendulum swung. Now our brains have been jogged. There it is, our pride. We'd been looking for that. The patriots are back in style. Hmm. What d'ya know? Guys who put their lives on the line are pretty cool, after all. Way to go, Grandpa.

This year, there will be more flag-waving, flag-wearing (!), song-singing new patriots than ever. I hope they don't ever get burned out like before.

Pardon me Roy, Is that the Cat that Chewed Your New Shoes?
My daughter said she's buying me new shoes for Mother's Day. "Can I have the money for that, Mom?" She says "You have more shoes than you have friends, and you need a new pair." Not really. I know who my friends are.

I bought my PF Flyers at Wal-Mart about 19 years ago. They're comfy. They will help me run fast, if I ever have occasion to run. I haven't yet, but it's nice knowing I'm prepared. I have a pair of dress shoes which I bought 8 years ago at a thrift store for two dollars, and a pair of boots that I wore in high school. That's three (count 'em) pairs of shoes. That's it.

They are comfy and only a little scuffed. Why only three? I guess I got embarrassed by the Imelda Marcos fiasco. No, not really. I just feel comfortable with what I have. No, that's not it either . All the shoes in my size are ugly. Nope, that's not it either . I guess I'm just unwilling to spend more than what I paid so many years ago for shoes. Hear the little birdies saying, "Cheap, cheap." No, that couldn't be it. I guess its a rebellion thing. I am the kid who used to go barefoot from the day school was out in June until they forced me to put my feet in those nasty Oxfords for the following school year.

Parking lots become much bigger in summertime if you are barefoot. But it's easier to climb trees and play hide and seek if you don't have to wear clunky old school shoes. The only time I wore shoes in the summertime is when we played stickball, and then I wore (surprise) PF Flyers. Just how old is too old for footwear?

What could it mean if your shoes are older than your new lover? They say it is a "woman thing" to buy and hoard shoes. Well, if all others around you are buying shoes and you would rather read a book or go to a movie, is your femininity questionable?

I know that I don't buy things for myself because I am a mom. Typically, I will spend my last dime on my kids or grandkids before I get my own allergy pills or a box of Kleenex. I will forego my own health to purchase new Pokemon shoes for my grandson. This sort of self-sacrifice is a behavior of many moms, not just me. That's why mother and martyr sound similar.

I don't want shoes as a present, either. I would rather have flowers, candy, gold, diamonds, cash, but shoes -I don't think so. Now about that new pair of friends, hmm.

Well, that won't happen either. Reporters don't typically have friends. Everyone is too cautious to even talk to a reporter like a real person. We can't have a conversation without hearing "This is off the record" or "Don't print this." Oh, like I would tell the world about your politics.

Anyway, for Mother's Day, I am getting a computer and a big hug from my best friend (who is older than my shoes), a phone call from my grandchildren, and a trip to the Wal-Mart shoe department with my daughter. She needs new sandals.

A Non-Martha Feast

Does anyone ever forget the stress of making a beautiful Thanksgiving Dinner for all the relatives? In my decorated past, I had been responsible for the Martha Stewart feast my family had come to rely on each November.

I fumbled a bit.

I am a great turkey chef, and I can make sweet potato pie, chestnut dressing, and pumpkin cheesecake, too. But it took a long time to learn everything. It is a frantic process in the kitchen the day before and the morning of Thanksgiving. You have to let the bird swim in the sink overnight so he'll be ready to burn the next day, and freak out about making all the other stuff that can be made ahead of time and you have to have more counter space and you never have all the correct tools.

Why does the turkey-baster disappear each year? It was there last week. Plus you have to wash the dust off of the turkey platter with some heavy-duty chemical and make sure you have complete place settings. I wonder how Martha keeps churning out lovely centerpieces when I always had to worry about matching silverware. My dishwasher ate forks, and someone was always using a butter knife as a screwdriver. My kids always took spoons out into the back yard and they broke literally tons of glassware.

We were going to have to resort to jelly jars one year, but luckily, Mom bought me an early Christmas present of matching glasses. So the table never did look exactly like Martha's, but at least everyone will have a fork and a jelly jar. I never got around to a colorful centerpiece.

Then there's the matter of enough chairs around the table so you get the broken office chair out of the den and the piano bench for the twins, drag the recliner to the head of the table and don't forget the step ladder, in case some extra cousin shows up.

When my son was little, he was a handful in the kitchen. Actually, he was two and a half handfuls and could have been launched, via boot, out the back door, if I'd had a mind to do it. I remember a recipe I wrote back then called How to Bake a Cake...see if it takes you back. You will need: large mixing bowl, flour, eggs, sugar, baking soda, salt, a little milk, softened butter, vanilla, a greased baking pan, a camera and Prozac.

Directions:
Preheat oven to 350.

THE VANILLA PEOPLE

Sift flour into mixing bowl.
Add in sugar, slowly.
Answer phone.
Come back to cake mixture.
Remove Jack's sticky hands from bowl.
Remove toy cars from flour.
Wash table, Rinse Jack's hands.
Dump flour, Re-sift new flour and dry ingredients together.
Get eggs out of refrigerator.
Turn and catch bowl as Jack knocks the cake mixture off the table.
Sweep flour mixture off floor, re-sift new ingredients.
Chase Jack around kitchen to retrieve eggs.
Mop up egg accident. Wash Jack.
Add eggs to mixture.
Notice lizard tail sticking out of Jack's pocket. Look for more lizards around kitchen.
Dump cake and lizard mixture. Wash bowl. Re-sift flour. Add eggs and milk.
Hear giggles and turn to see Jack feeding the dog the butter.
Put dog outside. Wash Jack. Look for more butter in the refrigerator.
Turn just in time to see bowl crash to floor, dumping mixture on Jack's head.
Take picture of Jack covered in cake dough.
Dump mixture, wash table, Jack, floor.
Take pill. Put Jack down for nap.
Re-sift dry ingredients. Add eggs, milk, butter, vanilla. Pour batter into pan.
Open oven, find the last lizard, lightly browned.
Dump the lizard and the cake mix into the trash.
Call bakery. Lie down.
One Thanksgiving I offered to make the turkey at my cousin's house. I bought a 28- pounder and discovered just prior to baking

time that it didn't quite fit in the oven. We stuffed it in there anyway, and the top of the bird burned black, scraping across the top of the oven. I was teased unmercifully, and it left a bad taste in my mouth. So did the turkey.

Men, if there's one thing you can do for your women who pour their hearts into this meal for you, it's DON'T tease. Say it tastes wonderful, even if it was an experiment in terror. The last thing you need is a cook in tears the day before the biggest shopping day of the year. This year, no tears. I'm happy just to contribute a cheesecake. Let someone else worry about broken forks. I'm going to put an olive on each fingertip and sit at the kid table.

Keep Your Salad to Yourself

We used to have the Norman Rockwell kind of Thanksgiving, with the big family all salivating over a huge turkey, little kids at the kid table, black olives stuck on the end of each finger. There would always be the strange aunt, who arrived late and brought a covered dish, which everyone had just prayed she wouldn't bring. It was usually something sour, hot and foreign, and it could be found after Thanksgiving, spat into the planters.

Perhaps the spitters thought half-chewed stuffed grape leaves might take root and be useful one day. Since everybody grew up and moved away, the family tradition has changed and its a lot more like Picasso than Rockwell. Now one person cooks the turkey and dressing, and everyone else brings "a covered dish." There aren't enough planters, let me tell you.

The reason it brings to mind Picasso, is there are a lot of repeat dishes. Even though we carefully coordinate who is going to bring what, everyone brings something extra and it's usually a duplicate, like Picasso's five or six hands, eyes or noses. With us, the problem was green salads. I think one year, about 30 years ago, someone forgot to make a salad. We haven't let it go yet.

I know the whole idea is to be grateful for having enough food for winter, and we should be thankful we have relatives who care enough to bring their special recipe, but as often as I've prayed for no one to bring carrot-raisin salad, you'd think God would heed such a request. Nope. He must be trying to teach me a valuable lesson. Perhaps tolerance.

In fact, if a prayer goes up on the Wednesday before Thanksgiving for Aunt Lois to never bring those cement blocks she calls hot rolls again, you can be sure she'll be there with the dreaded rolls and a new recipe she found in a magazine, for apricot glazed shredded goat's brain casserole. The rolls have to be placed carefully on the table, or they will topple it. The casserole, well, it looks like somebody already ate it. But I'm tolerant.

Here is a list of food items I don't want to see, but I'm not going to pray about it. I'm just going to wish really hard.

Homemade turtle soup. (Someone in my Dad's family actually tried this.)

Ribbon salad. This is tri-level Jell-o, with fruit suspended in two of the flavors. It seems to be more in line with a science project.

Fruitcake. Ick.

Stuffed grape leaves. Unfortunately, "it's all Greek" to the chef.

Pizza. Come on. The turkey's not that dry.

Carrot/Raisin salad. I want to know who thought of this atrocity. The kind with Jell-o added is no better.

Lima beans. (I'm allergic.)

Any pie made with rhubarb or mincemeat.

Aunt Verla's Cauliflower/head cheese casserole. Once is enough.

Liver and okra. (A family favorite, except for me.)

I'll eat spinach. I'll eat yams. I'll eat fuzzy green beans. I'll even eat popcorn & toast. Just don't subject me to your experimental Thanksgiving treats. Let me get up and watch the Macy's parade, wave to Santa & have a light breakfast of grits and hot apple cider. Then I'll make a green salad and a pumpkin pie, and maybe a coconut cream pie and get ready to go to a 4 p.m. "dinner" at Nana & Papa's house.

I will be the crazy aunt with the awesome desserts. (No one has ever spit my pie into a planter.) We'll sit around the well-stocked table with enough green salad to feed six armies and say what we're thankful for this year, and someone will invariably say, I'm thankful that no one brought that cauliflower stuff. Then the doorbell will ring, and everyone will hold his or her breath. It will be Aunt Jeni, with her famous chocolate fudge, and another salad, just in case anyone forgot. We'll all shout Hooray! All the aunts will have arrived, and there will be nothing sinister, deadly or glazed on the table. That is my holiday wish.

All I Want for Christmas Is...

I got a scribble in the mail. It was a letter from my granddaughter. She's two, and she was obviously telling me what she wanted for Christmas. I asked her father exactly what doll she wanted, and he said, "Mom, we live in Texas now. She doesn't want a doll. She's into guns." I was silent for a moment. He said, "It's a joke, Mom." It better be. She already has a temper problem. I told him I'd forward a copy of her request to Santa.

Since I was four, I have written letters to Santa regarding my list of needs and wants and quite a few of my desires have been met. I usually wrote the letters in November, just after Thanksgiving, and was surprised one year when a store Santa asked, "What do you want for Christmas, little girl?" I said, "Didn't you get my note?" He said he hadn't checked the mail but he was sure I'd get what was coming to me.

I never got a lump of coal, but I got the same doll two years in a row. In 1966, my sisters and I got an extraordinary amount of stuff. Included in my wonderful stuff was a beautiful blonde doll in a cheery flowered dress. It was my favorite present. Unfortunately, it didn't last long. By the end of the day after Christmas, being snowed in, Mom was tired of tripping over boxes and dolls and trucks and other toys. She said if we didn't pick up our stuff we'd lose it forever.

We went to sleep with a scattering of toys on the floor. When we woke up, the floor was clean. My precious doll was gone, nowhere to be found. I even looked in the garbage, thinking Mom tossed it. It wasn't there. It had disappeared from the face of the earth. My older sister lost a record, and my younger sister lost a stuffed dog.

Mom never claimed responsibility for the missing toys. She gave the impression that she thought the toys had vanished in response to our negligence -some kind of cosmic rip in the universe. Well, we gave up the search as 1966 turned into 1967, and we were a little cleaner that year. The seasons came and went, and then it was Christmas time again. I wrote Santa that if he brought me a doll like I had last year, I promised to take better care of it.

Lo and behold, Christmas morning, that same doll was under the tree for me, along with Annette's Beatle record and Jeni's stuffed puppy. It was a miracle. For the first time, I thought, Wow! I can write totally effective business letters. I was going to hone that skill.

Through the years, I have asked for and received: front teeth, a bicycle with a banana seat, ice skates, a puppy, a kitty, a fuzzy purple sweater and a Mrs. Beasley doll. I also asked for: no more freckles, the end of world hunger, and the cancellation of the Donny and Marie show. No, no, yes! I have asked for big things, like a car that works every day, and a TV that you don't have to use pliers on to change the channel. That would almost be better than the yacht and the mink.

One time, Santa sent a crib for my baby, whom I brought home Christmas Eve 1977, and all the time I was thinking I'd have to keep him in a box. Oh, I'd poke holes in the top and throw in some lettuce, I was thinking. But it wasn't necessary. Santa had come through again, just like with my Mrs. Beasley.

I once made an unusual request, that diamond/ruby Wonder-Bra. Mom always let us open one present on Christmas Eve. Inevitably it was socks or underwear. Just once, Santa could have made that exciting.

I have couched some requests in altruism. I asked for my family to get along better, for my friend not to be sick, and please, Santa, how about an all-expense paid vacation for five to Disney World. You kind of have to pad the list to get at least one thing on it. That's the way Santa works.

This year I'm going to request world peace, an extra day in each weekend, and a full college scholarship for my daughter -I hope to get at least one of those small requests, because I believe in Santa. And he likes the way I write.

The Twisted Twelve

I have a question for you. Why is it that every year, we mindlessly keep singing the 12 Days of Christmas without giving a thought to the math? Well, let me tell you, I have done all the calculations and this song is a MESS. First, how many people celebrate all 12 days, or even know what those days are, exactly? Well, it begins Christmas Day and goes through January 6th. Ok, most people take the tree down before the 6th. On January 5th, most people are just sitting around waiting for Valentines Day. All those people should stop singing on or about the 7th day.

Now supposedly, this song is a tribute from a woman to a man....her true love, who gave her a plethora of presents one year. And she's like..."Wrote a song about it, wanna hear it? Here it goes." It starts out pretty cute...sing along with me, On the first day of Christmas, my true love gave to me, a partridge in a pear tree.

That's nice. A bird, a place to keep it, and maybe a little fruit on the side. Then the next day, the doorbell rings, and there's the UPS guy with a couple more birds..."On the second day of Christmas my true love gave to me, two turtle doves AND a partridge in a pear tree." Well the first partridge must have been lonely. So now she's got 3 birds, two trees and an unknown number of pears. This is the point in the song where Mom leans over to Dad and says, "You never get me nuthin like that."

Suddenly its the dawning of a new day. "On the third day of Christmas, my true love gave to me, three french hens, two turtle doves and a partridge in a pear tree." That makes 10 birds and three trees. What a nice man, that true love. Funny, there should have been a cage…

Day Four: She's singing "On the Fourth Day of Christmas, my true love gave to me." let me guess, another bird? Yep. Four of them, four calling birds. Plus three more french hens, two more turtle doves and a partridge in a pear tree. Thats a bird count of 20, and four trees, plus a lot of pears. Can you imagine the phone call that night? "Hello, Brian, Wow, Thank you SO much for all the birds. Yeah, you know my friend, Pam? Her boyfriend went to Jared. Yeah. Jewelry, uh huh. Can you imagine? What a great gift idea for the holidays."

Then its day five. On the Fifth Day of Christmas, my true love gave to me….FIVE GOLD RINGS! Woohoo! You think its a reprieve, don't ya? But just for good measure, and to flesh out the lyrics, he threw in four more calling birds, three more French hens, two more turtle doves, and another partridge in another pear tree. By now, this lady's neighbors have filed a noise grievance with the landlord. I think I'd be getting just the slightest bit annoyed with my true love about now, wouldn't you?

On the sixth day of Christmas, my true love gave to me, again with the birds…SIX geese, a'laying. That means hatching some eggs. Oh joy. Plus, five more rings, four more calling birds, three more French hens, two more turtle doves, and a partridge in a pear tree. That means inside this lady's apartment are 46 birds, 10 gold rings, 6 trees, plus an untold number of pears and eggs. Hope Mom sends an omelet pan.

On the seventh day of Christmas, I'd be so nervous when the doorbell rang. And there's the UPS guy, by now our lady is like…"Hi Sam. Come on in." He's got helpers, as he delivers seven swans, a'swimming. The song never says what they are swimming in, so I imagine each swan is in its own self-contained pool. From Sharper Image. And along with those swans, Sam brings in six more geese a'laying, five more rings, four more calling birds, three French hens, two turtle doves, and another partridge in a pear tree. That makes the count 69 birds, 15 gold rings, and seven trees plus x number of eggs and pears. From her TRUE LOVE. Should have registered at Macy's.

On the eighth day of Christmas, my true love gave to me....one huge migraine, I'd think, if I answered the door and there were 8 girls milking 8 cows. This is undoubtedly where the phrase "Its just what I always wanted" originated. Along with the girls and their cows, there are seven more swans a'swimmin, six more geese a'layin, 5 more rings, four more calling birds, three more French hens, two more turtle doves, and another partridge in a pear tree. By now, even the gold jewelry doesn't make up for the noise or the mess of 92 birds, or the lack of fruit variety.

On the ninth day of Christmas, what will he think of next? OH, of Course! nine ladies, dancing. Probably all with their own boom-boxes. Yeah, how do you know my true love, sister? Ok. Whatever...want some scrambled eggs and milk? Wait. Make room for 8 more girls and 8 more cows, (I used to have nice neighbors.) seven more swans swimming like mad, six more geese, five more rings, four more calling birds, three more French hens, two more turtle doves, and another partridge in a pear tree.

On the 10th day of Christmas, there are 10 guys leaping about outside. This is clearly a gift. From her true love. Perhaps they leap because they are joined by nine more dancing ladies, 8 more gals with cows, seven more swans, six more geese, five more rings, four more calling birds, three more French hens (ooo la la) two more turtle doves, and a partridge in a pear tree. Do you suppose this lady's name is Mary? Mary, did you know...how to get a restraining order?

On the 11th day of Christmas, my true love gave to me....11 pipers, piping. Because what you want to hear when you have 171 birds in your house....I said because what you want to hear when you have one hundred seventy one birds in your house, is a jaunty little tune on the bagpipes. "Yeah, officer, there are 10 more guys in tights leaping about, nine more ladies to dance with them, 8 more girls with 8 more cows, yes, my psyche HAS become fragile, seven more swans, six more geese on the nest, five more rings, four more calling birds—by the way, who are they calling?—three more French hens, two more turtle doves, and another partridge in a pear tree.

Sing it. On the 12th day of Christmas…what is that noise I hear? Is it the men in white coats? No, its 12 drummers, drumming, along with 11 more guys with bagpipes, 10 more lords leaping about on the lawn, nine more ladies dancing (in case the first 27 got tired) 8 more maids a'milking, 7 more swans swimming, six more geese laying, 5 more gold rings—enough to put two on every finger and toe—four more calling birds, three more French hens, two more turtle doves, and yet another partridge in yet another pear tree. That's just about the whole Partridge family, wouldn't you say?

At the end of the 12th day, no wonder they call it Epiphany. Now you're going to bring this up in your math class, aren't you? Our friend Mary has accumulated 12 drummers, 22 pipers, 66 dancers, 40 maids, 40 cows, 42 swans in 42 individual allergy-free swimming containers, 42 geese. 40 gold rings, 36 calling birds, 30 French hens, 22 turtle doves, 12 partridges, 12 pear trees plus the innumerable eggs and pears. That's 194 birds and 140 people—and its hard to wrap people.

If Mary is like me, she is making a new checklist.

1. Send thank-you card to true love. Tell him you'll be singing his praises for years to come.
2. Give landlord a big box of pears.
3. Hold a cow sale.
4. Send a few—no, send one of those leaping lords to sister.
5. Donate a majority of birds to the local zoo.
6. Get to the bottom of that rumor about milkmaid # 17
7. Have extra session with therapist.
8. Hock a couple of rings.
9. Explain gift certificates to true love.

10. Spend next Christmas with Sam from UPS.

Finally, when all is said and done, and all the bird mess is piled up in the corner, Mary is likely thinking of a different song. I could be wrong, but I think she might be humming 50 Ways to Leave Your Lover.

In a Twistmas Mood

To quote Ado Annie, "With or without the mistletoe, I'm in a holiday mood." I love Christmas, even though it means I'm another year older. I would sing "Jingle Bells" all year long, if the kids didn't threaten to call the men in white coats. Sometimes when I'm alone, I watch "It's A Wonderful Life" or "Miracle on 34th Street" in the middle of July.

My Christmas tree went up Thanksgiving night. I am playing my Chipmunk Christmas CD daily. I'll tell you a secret. Every year, the Santa that is in the Macy's Thanksgiving Day Parade is the real Santa. He sees me when I wave from the TV audience, and he always waves back. "They" always fault me for being a believer.

There's nothing wrong with my belief system. I believe in God, and heaven and angels and I hope to walk streets of gold one day. I hope there are no cracks in the sidewalk up there. Some folks would say I can't believe in God AND Santa, because their holidays are diametrically opposed. Santa espouses commercialism, where Jesus' birth was a divine act.

I tell these people that I'm glad that both Jesus and Santa felt like sharing my birthday. I also believe in Cupid, the Tooth Fairy, leprechauns, the Easter beagle and the Great Pumpkin. I'm not cynical about anything mystical. I think the toys come to life when we're not looking, and animals have secret meetings to discuss taking over.

Lily Tomlin as Edith Ann said, "Do you think God is watching us? I think so. He has a TV set -he watches us on it. Whenever I think he's watching me I always sing and dance and do a commercial for myself." I have taken this advice to heart. I believe in other legends, too. Rudolph, Frosty, the Grinch. It's all good.

I also believe in the dark side. There are witches and demons, but they are not welcome to spend the holidays with me.

On the other hand, Santa always eats the cookies and milk we leave out for him. There is, for the past 40 years, a gift under our tree that mysteriously appears, and no one in the house knows where it came from, except I know it came from the North Pole, special delivery. My Grandma Savage was a devout Baptist. She never put up with any nonsense. So when she cut a piece of cake for Santa, I knew he was real.

One time when I was 6, she sat me down and told me that I have a gift. I said, "There are 5 presents under the tree for me." She said, "You also have the invisible gift of faith." She said my faith was strong and she hoped it lasted me a lifetime. I believe it will. It bothers me that others don't believe, or they tell their kids there's no such thing as Santa Claus. But I won't push their buttons.

I am not one to poke holes in the balloons of my birthday guests. Some of them believe in Bigfoot, or the Loch Ness Monster. And some still believe in truth, justice and the American Way.

Missive Mania

Every year, I write a Christmas Missive to the members of my ancestral family, the Savages of Texas, Mississippi, Nevada and other miscellaneous states. It is a tradition sparked by my aunts, Marj and Nita, who wait a whole year and write down the highlights and the accomplishments of their families, while the rest of us wait with bated bad breath.

Who's married, divorced, grown a beard, moved, graduated, joined the Navy or the circus, danced naked on the courthouse steps, these are the things we show and tell in our loving Christmas missives. But it's not gossip. Because I have grown so attached to Willows, I will now include y'all in my Missive list.

Here is a little preparation…everyone in my family has a silent j in their name, or they would like one. They all come from a Baptist/

fundamentalist upbringing, yet only my Mom attends church regularly. Also, rather than spout about my family's real accomplishments, I make them up, but don't tell my mom. Anyway, it starts out.

Dear Ancestral Savages, and those with or without silent J's, As you may have guessed, this is the annual missive from that famous writer, Joie Roblin, here on earth to enlighten y'all with bits and pieces of this journey we call life. (You have to throw in a couple of y'alls with my family, or they think you're get tin' too fancy.)

I write this passage in the November of my discontent. The days are colder and wintry winds blast through the Sacramento Valley, with rain and fog and bitter cold wreaking havoc on the roads, as the winter season hits sunny California. 1999 has been a year of changes and challenges.

We got full-time custody of H IS children, and so we have become a blended family and I have been listed on the school enrollment cards as the evil stepmother. They are great kids, but I am trying to change that.

We are somehow happy and peaceful. We moved and blended into a house, with four bedrooms and two living rooms. Uptown! We have a washer and dryer that don't require quarters. Here's the challenge part -our oven is the size of an Easy Bake Oven for a dollhouse.

Another change was in my employment. As most of you know, in March I became a reporter for the Willows Journal. It is an awesome job. I am not just a reporter, but also a photojournalist and columnist, and comic relief. Of course, I am also beloved by the Willows residents.

The challenge here is the 120-mile daily commute, over country roads full of skunk and raccoon road kill. I once hit a low-flying pheasant. It was coming right for me. Luckily, I had my trusty blue Hyundai.

More family change...I became a Grandmama for the second time, and it wasn't any easier. Lots of labor pains. My wonderful granddaughter has reddish blonde hair and she screams when I hold her. She only likes her Dad. We figure her two-year-old brother must be one of us, because he is a Star Trek fan and a Jeopardy enthusiast. Definitely Savage.

Anyway, thanks to Buddha, they moved from the ghetto to Willows, becoming part of my growing fan club. My daughter just turned 16. To acknowledge her survival skills, a party was held in the garage, where several teenagers damaged their hearing and gyrated like demons in hell to what they called "music." No police had to be summoned.

Anyway, she is beautiful and sweet and she got 4 A's on her report card. She also has a boyfriend. (He is scared of me.) Of course, she will have to stop all that being wonderful stuff when she formally joins the cult. They plan to shave her head and arms, pierce her belly button and teach her backwards, guttural language of the Dark Leader. Don't discourage her. If she doesn't join, then I have to teach her how to drive.

These and many other changes have been thrust upon us this year. We like most of them. We are all looking forward to 2000, because it isn't here yet. We wish you all a Merrjy Christjmas and a Happjy JNew Yjear.

Missive 2000

Once again, here is my annual missive to my friends and family and adoptive hometown, Willows. My family expects a couple of "y'all's" and references to my scandalous black sheep nature. I give y'all my poetry.

Dear Ancestors and others who love me: Greetings from this fog-enveloped small town; If you're ever in California, come on down. It's Christmas time, we're all happy as elves; we're smiling so much we don't seem like ourselves.

In my little apartment, I have a house full of kids; today on each one I'm holding open bids. I am still with the Journal, a job I hold dear; I make a fortune with my pen, but the bank says my checks don't clear.

My son and his family have moved here from Reno; obviously tired of slot machines and Keno. My daughter is a junior at Willows High School; She's in choir and drama and everybody says she's cool.

Calvin the Fantastic is my grandson and my buddy; he can't help it if he goes outside and comes back in all muddy. His little sister, Cori, screams and yells all night and day; It's her job to yell gibberish -she has important things to say.

Cori's hair is kind of short, but long enough for Grandma to braid; She yells, I braid, she yells, I braid, it's the game that must be played. We have a dog, two cats, a mouse and three fish; the pets entertain because we can't afford a satellite dish.

The love of my life lives far away in another small town near Sac; we broke up in March but we're still in love, it was never love we lacked. So I moved from his house to this little place and stopped my long commutes; this is the home of the Lamb Derby fest, but I still miss the Sutter Buttes.

The event of the year was when Ma and Pa had their Golden Wedding Anniversary; Friends & family came from miles around to say, "You're still together? Have mercy!" To top off the celebration, I had to wreck my car; with my favorite teenagers in it, the Hyundai didn't get far.

We all survived and I got a new auto to drive from there to here; all those screams and the freeway is something I fear. We haven't had much of a scandal and no one got married or changed churches; No arrests, no court dates, no fortunes made, no radical extravagant purchases.

We all want to be millionaires, we get all the answers right; but being from Vanilla stock, I'm afraid there'd be a fight. Right on the stage, with Regis we'd fight, Yes A's my final answer; "Well, you're wrong, he'd say, the answer is B, the second reindeer is Dancer."

Family members would rush the stage and yell at the contestant cousin; Probably slap Regis, jump up and down and start the audience buzzin'. It wouldn't be a pretty scene, in fact it would be pretty rude; we'd likely be selected to play a round of Family Feud.

I'll stay right here and work on my book if y'all don't mind; when it's all done, I'll send you a copy and I'll make sure it's signed. In the meantime, Merry Christmas, Happy New Year from all of us; we wish y'all would come see us take a plane or a bus. You'd like it here in Willows. I'll introduce you to Glenn County's best; Y'all come on out this summer you cain't beat the Golden West.

Another Poetic Missive

Hey, folks! It is time once again for the annual letter to my Savage ancestors and friends, whom I ignore during the rest of the year. The family calls it "The Annual Christmas Missive Exchange."

I have a million relatives, half of them with the middle name Jo, and they all live in a trailer park and have a southern accent and a Ford. They vote Republican, except for

Aunt Marj.

They yearn for information from Willows, California, which they think is next door to the ocean, and I'm just the Jo to let them know they're wrong. But in this campaign, my aunts & uncles & cousins compete to see who can write the best lies about their various lives. Conversely, my mother writes about the foliage around her home. She just doesn't get it.

I write about the enormous accomplishments and fantastic events that I experience. Obviously, my letters are brief.

Dear Savage relation or friend,

Happy Thanksgiving and Merry Christmas to all,

You owe me a letter, or at least a phone call.

This year's been chock-full of excitement and thrills,

In fact, the fun never stops, nor do the bills.

A monthly installment is due every day, and you'd think I have more stuff to show for what I have to pay.

I often go on and on about how I have no money; but its true I'm dead broke and its less and less funny.

Life's become a tragic comedy in an epileptic state; I need Prozac when the mail comes or I tend to cry, of late.

I think in rhyme like Dr. Seuss but my themes are all subjective; I'm tired, I'm old, I'm very poor and I'm losing my objective.

Luckily I have a job and my skills are not too old and funky; I have a warning sign on my desk 'don't make me get my flying monkeys.'

In January, February, and even March not much happened but the weather; the formidable aunts came to visit but we didn't spend enough time together.

In April and May it got pretty hot, we melted and had a lamb derby fest; in June and July and August too, we continued to melt -its called an endurance test.

September and school started up too soon, and then the whole terrorist thing; but it brought out the best in the people and the nation stood up to sing.

Though we're cynical about some folks and their newfound flag-waving pride; it's heartwarming to see us all pull together and it's about time we tried.

September was also the beginning of my baby's senior year;

She's 18 and gorgeous and will set the world on its ear.

When she goes off to college I'll be alone; how sad it is when your children grow up and your parenting skills are still unknown. My son moved away; packed his kids and left town; From Willows to Phoenix to Reno to Texas but now he's settled down. I miss those grandbabies with a terrible sorrow; by the time I get to see them it will be a thousand tomorrows.

We have Kismet and Karma and now a new cat; Ophelia the Tabby, who makes me want a baseball bat. The mischief factor of two cats and a dog; I can't tell you my feelings; my glasses have fogged.

A long distance romance still keeps my heart from freezing; he's the one who makes me laugh and gives me pills when I'm sneezing. Just two more months in "Oh, one" to go, the holidays are here; hop in your car and come see us, we'll take you out for root beer. Don't make me go another year without seeing your Savage face; at least sit down and answer this missive -the first Jo to write wins the race.

CHRISTMAS MISSIVE 2008, OR, THEN I MOVED TO TEXAS

Dear Ancestors & Friends,

Congratulations! You are the lucky recipient of my annual Christmas missive, in which is detailed description and narrative of my most exciting life. Yes folks, Coffee City is a happenin' place. The grass grows in winter. I've been here just a bit more than a year, and already I've met a few neighbors. They seem just like family.

I found a great job this year. Of course, I did have to sign up to become Catholic, but I have fun every day at Trinity Mother Frances Hospital. It was named for this chick who came to the US from Poland in the late 1800s, but never actually moved to Texas. I wish the citizens of France would name the Eiffel Tower after me, because I've never been there.

Everyone here is fine, but they say it is heck growing older. Miss Jane turned 5 in October, despite the warning, and she says "It rocks when you be five." I've decided to be five on my birthday, too, because I want to rock.

People have asked what it is like to live in East Texas. Here is the definitive statement. Every morning the clouds rest on Lake Palestine, dusting the eye with the illusion of a hot lake giving off steam. Take what you will from that.

On any lazy Saturday you can sit on Mom's porch and watch the beauty of nature, as thousands of Cousin Loren's cats roam Pinedale Lane. These are the cats Loren keeps in his basement, with the boxes marked "Syria" or "Korea." In the evening, choose a trailer. There will be an aunt with a card game in progress. They will cheat.

On Sunday afternoons, for amusement, or therapy, you can stand out in the street and see who can yell the loudest. Dad is the judge. Then Mom will fix you a taco. Now I say Saturday or Sunday, but really, the calendar has no meaning in East Texas, other than marking the day the nurse visits, or to note when some relative might come over for a week. This so rarely occurs that we are trying to find another stray, rabid dog to bite one of us for the entertainment value. Aunt Nita, come back!

There is a kind of space and time anomaly that happens when you're here, just like when Captain Kirk got accelerated. {All Savage Christmas missives must contain a Star Trek reference} Some of the people move so slow, it is like they're standing still. Some are a little faster, but they're still on the same story they were telling last week. Then the children come by and they're buzzing around like big 'ol Texas insects—well, they're not as big as the insects, but you get the idea. There are about 6 neighborhood children, or just two that move really fast.

This was a tough year, as we lost part of the Fab Four. I miss Aunt Marj so much! It was great to see some cousins at her memorial. I wish we had more time together. I miss being around you. We need to have a cousin convention.

However, I am in great demand, having done excellent stand-up comedy at school, church, and the hospital cafeteria. You should not try to live your life vicariously through such a huge celebrity as me. Although you'd undoubtedly be breathless with awe, the pace would hurt you. Just endure as though you'll see me again soon.

Please have a wonderful 2009, and keep me in your prayers and your MySpace Top 8. As you prosper in the new year, remember to feel sorry for Mick and I daily, as we have to live so far away from each other for an undisclosed amount of time. After you weep, send us positive thoughts and ask Jesus to place us under the one roof very soon for an even longer undisclosed amount of time.

Until we see each other again and you bask in my glory,
Merry Christmas.

'Tis the Season for Getting OLD

It might be a little early, but my house is already decorated for

THE VANILLA PEOPLE

Christmas—we'll put the tree up right after Thanksgiving, probably that night. I have all my Christmas CDs out and I keep a running tune—Jingle Bells—in my head. I have more Christmas spirit than almost anyone except for whoever thought up that annoying dancing toy Santa. Have you seen it over there in the Christmas section at Wal-Mart? It could make a saint go postal.

But even though I love this time of year, I have four family birthdays this week. I have to think about how old everyone is getting, and uh-oh, it's starting to affect my Christmas spirit. It's starting to be the winter of my discontent.

The strangest thing has occurred this November. I've discovered I'm a little more than half the age of my dad and a little more than twice the age of my daughter. Twilight zone. My baby is 18 this week. It doesn't seem possible, since I just turned 18 last week. My dad is turning 75. How could that be, I wonder? He said he feels like he just turned 18 a couple weeks ago.

The problem is that I am so sexy and ageless. Darn these youthful good looks! People tell me all the time I don't look old enough to have a 23 year old son, much less grandchildren. I tell them I had him when I was 5 or 6. It was a miracle. That's why his initials are JC.

And the older my kids get, the younger I was when I had them. Pretty soon, I will have been born pregnant. Call the Enquirer. And those grandchildren? Well, yes I am too young to have them. Luckily, we communicate on the same level. Madonna and Tina Turner and Cher are all ageless beauties, and hmmm, all older than me.

I refuse to age gracefully. I was very upset about turning 40 and 41. Now I'm in total panic that I'll be 42 this Christmas. It is simply not possible; although my daughter keeps telling- me how old I am, over and over and over again, until it numbs my teeth. My long teeth.

I think this is the age when most people go absolutely bananas. Forty-two is a big black stinky number, and I don't want to go. It seems horrendously old and grandmother-ish and makes me want to get pierced or tattooed or at least color my hair with strawberry kiwi Kool-Aid. No one ever looks forward to turning 42, do they? Not like they look forward to turning 6.

I am not just bananas. What I really am is an old child. I play with dolls and trucks either with my grandchildren or without. I watch cartoons whenever I can, even skipping the news to do so. I love to play hopscotch and jump rope and freeze tag. I like to eat with my fingers. I love peanut butter and jelly. I spend an inordinate amount of time at Toys-R-Us. I like to wear my hair in pigtails and stick my tongue out at mean people. This is just not typical 42-year-old behavior.

My 18-year-old acts older than do. My grandson asked me how old I was—After a long day I told him I felt like I was 100. I might have a few years to shape up and start acting my age, but I probably will not use this time wisely. I just want to keep having fun. We are having fun, aren't we?

I think of other famous writers who had to be 42 at least once, and they can be counted on to become sorta twisted and bitter after thinking about how old they were. Dorothy Parker was about 40 when she wrote "Men seldom make passes at girls who wear glasses." Mark Twain was probably 42 when he wrote, "Reports of my death are greatly exaggerated."

In his 40's, Henry David Thoreau wrote "The mass of men lead lives of quiet desperation." And talk about a black mood, Edgar Allen Poe died at age 40, after he wrote, 'this fever called 'living' is conquered at last.'

William Shakespeare was just 52 when he died. When he was about 42, he wrote Hamlet, in which he declares something is rotten in the state of Denmark. I agree. In just about a month, I will have to turn 42, no matter how I object. Angels and ministers of grace, defend us.

And a Twisty New Year

Everybody says Happy New Year, as if they expect you to be

happy for the next 365 days, no matter what. I am more realistic.

Here are 31 ways to have at least part of one happy day (an afternoon, maybe) in the New Year. That's at least one opportunity per day per month. Now it's up to you.

Let a sales clerk have a piece of your mind.

Kick a tire.

Say "invisible" instead of "indivisible" during the Pledge of Allegiance.

Eat two desserts.

Throw an egg on the floor.

Kiss 10 people in one day.

Line up your pets and lecture them about drugs.

Drink out of the wrong side of a glass in public.

Sing loudly while walking down the street.

During every conversation ask, "Are you joking?"

Think about your goals now, and those from when you were in second grade. See if they've varied much.

Learn a new acronym every day.

Sign a bank deposit in crayon.

Place your lips on a window and blow. It makes a funny face.

Watch a Disney movie without the kids.

Spell everything phonetically (fon-etik-ly) in your next memo.

Play Monopoly, and when you land on a Railroad, yell "Chugga-Chugga-Choo-Choo!" and run around the room like a train.

Speak Pig Latin on the phone.

Sneeze on someone you dislike when you have a cold. Tell them you're spreading germs of cheer.

Buy a duck.

Write down all the zones you can think of.

Pretend a monster is coming.

Put a big plastic tooth under your pillow and tell the kids it's worth a fortune.

Take a picture while your repairman is walking away.

Do the Twist, like you did last summer.

Buy a goldfish. Name it Festus.

Pick a day when every member of the family wears something tie-dyed.

Pay the date instead of the amount of your phone bill. Works best in January.

Throw a piece of chicken at your in-law.

Make faces at other people while grocery shopping. If they confront you, say, "Oh, I just can't stand the price of deviled ham these days."

Take two aspirin and keep away from children.

My resolutions for '01 are: Apply Cheese Whiz where needed; don't die. I like to keep them simple. No crap about losing 20 pounds and making life easier for others. Cheese Whiz and non-death will be good enough for me in the new millennium.

Chapter 25
TWISTED DEATH

When They Call Me an Immortal Writer, They Ain't Kiddin'...
I often write about mental health issues, probably because I am one. I do not write to offend, but to inform. Warning: This is a dark ride.

I am immortal. I found this out long ago. The thing is, it is really hard to be suicidal when you're immortal. The best I can hope for is to get sick. I can't even do depression very well, because I keep laughing about how healthy I am. Is it mental illness or just another wacky day?

As a child, I used to climb trees, climb up on the roof, jump into the deep end of pools, pop wheelies on my bike and run barefoot across the supermarket parking lot and play rough games in the sand at the beach. I also used to fall out of trees & off the roof, get extreme allergic reactions to the chlorine in the pool, fall off my bike, get blisters and skinned knees from running across the parking lot and sustain third degree sunburns at the beach. (I have explosive Irish white skin.) But I never died.

As a morbid, black-wearing, Cooper worshipping teenager, I tried to commit suicide several times. It didn't work. I jumped out of a second story window. Nothing. Not a scratch. Ok, it wasn't a skyscraper. But there was only concrete underneath. And I walked away bewildered but not broken.

I drank poison. No result yet. I took pills. The only result was that I slept for 16 hours. I ran out in the middle of the road, hoping a car would run me over. There was no traffic. I waited an hour. Nothing.

I cut my wrists. They stopped bleeding, because I'm anemic. I've been in three car accidents, two skating accidents, about a thousand bike accidents, and I've had to run from a cloud of bees. Should have died. Survived.

I've been through an abusive marriage and a nasty divorce and raised two teenagers. Didn't die. I'm still here, drowning in bills, but that won't kill me either. I ought to get a cape, paint myself red and blue and call myself Super-Jo.

I guess it means I'm supposed to do something with my life. I have a purpose, which I believe has something to do with humor. Either that or I'm the suicidal twin of Wiley Coyote. Things ain't working out for either of us. I have not yet received my anvil from Acme.

So, though I may think thoughts of death, it does not become me, and I do not become it. An old friend once told me to think homicide rather than suicide, because we are put here on this earth to think of others before ourselves. I said I couldn't think of anyone I wanted to kill. At the time, I had not experienced a mother-in-law. Now I sort of lean toward that path-o-logic.

In fact, during certain times, I wish there were a local tower and an AK-47 dealership. Of course, then I would have to change Super-Jo to Killer-Jo, and get new business cards. Meanwhile, we're going to have to wait for that tower, until Economic Development does a feasibility study.

Mocking Death

Thoughts of my death are greatly exaggerated, in my own mind. It is somewhat understandable, given my propensity to wreck cars and my incredible old age. But guess what? Madonna is older than I.

In the Wizard Of Oz, Jack Haley said, "Some day they're going to erect a statue to me in this town." Auntie Em replied, "Well, don't start posing for it now." I am of the opinion that if a statue is in our future for any reason (I'm thinking headstone) we ought to be able to direct the sculpting. The founding fathers have been sculpted standing straight and tall, or riding a charging horse. Only Abraham Lincoln had the right idea. He is just sitting in a chair, relaxing. After standing in line at DMV for a third of my life, I want to be sculpted relaxed on the couch, remote in one hand, root-beer in the other.

Or I could pose on a chaise lounge in my sunglasses, surrounded by piles of money. Of course, it would be cement money, unspendable. Much like now.

This brings thoughts of how I want to die. Most people say the best way to go is in your sleep when you're of ancient age. That's ok, but I think I just want to be blown up. Strap me to the dynamite and push the detonator. Then they can say, "Boom. There she goes!" and there won't be anything left for burial or inurnment, so it eliminates funeral expenses. When I'm ready to go, they can just take me out on the lake and set me off with the fireworks. I will light up the sky. And this will be somewhat quaint, as I have brightened the day for so many people for so long.

In case some folks have the idea I should be mourned and there should be a memorial service with cake and coffee, I have a few requests.

Tell Weird AL I'll be waiting for him in the great beyond.

Tell each of my children separately that they were my favorite child.

Tell my ex-mother-in-law that my last words were a curse on her and her son.

Actually, my last words will probably be "Where did I put my keys?"

If the following music is played at my memorial service I will refuse to listen:

Macarena
Funkytown
Ma Na Ma Na
The Benny Hill Show theme
Happy Birthday
You Light Up My Life
The Barney Song
The theme from Gilligan's Island
The Union Label Song
Kum-Ba-Ya.

If these songs are played, I will hear, and I will come back and haunt whoever does it. I promise.

On our birthdays, when we were kids, my sisters and I used to pray, "Now I lay me down to sleep, I pray the Lord my soul will keep, If I should die before I wake, don't let my sister eat my birthday cake. Of course, we knew our lives on this earth were going to be short because we forgot to say the blessing for mealtimes when we were hungry. Then we'd remember, and say, "God is good, God is great. Please bless the food we already ate. And don't let it give us a bellyache."

I save the bits of wisdom that I like from fortune cookies, and I've never received one that said I would have a long life. Oh, sure, I will be awarded some great honor, I have an active mind and keen imagination, and my mentality is alert and analytical, yada, yada, yada. Long Life? Hello? Nothing. Of course my children then say, "Well, Mom, you've already had a long life."

Actually, I know the journey is not quite over, because I haven't paid off my credit cards or the phone bill, and I can't possibly die until I'm at least one dollar ahead. I guess that does mean a long life for me.

Ode to Stevie

I miss my little friend, Stevie Gilstrap. He was seven and I was six, and we were good buddies. He showed me how to hold a bat, and we would make faces at each other in Sunday school when the teacher wasn't looking. She always wondered what was so funny, because I was always giggling. Stevie made great faces.

One time I was at his house and we had played all of his games and we were bored. That's when he told me he had a cloud. He said he took an airplane ride with his dad in the crop duster and he reached out the window and grabbed a cloud and now he keeps it in his closet.

Being somewhat skeptical at age 6, I said, "Unh, unh." He said, "Yeah, huh."

"Unh, unh."

"Yeah, huh." This went on for some time, and then he offered to show me the cloud he kept in a paper bag in the closet. He got a chair to reach the shelf, and he reached into the dark and pulled out a little paper bompliment he could think of. "You're pretty strong, for a girl." I knew then that he loved me.

Stevie and his sister and I played Monopoly for six hours one rainy day, and I was winning when my parents wanted to leave. We were backing out of the driveway when Stevie came running out and said, "I'm glad you're leaving. I just landed on your Boardwalk." He leaned in the window and gave me my very first kiss. Right there in front of my Dad.

Stevie's life was much too short. He got leukemia in second grade, and his family moved to Arizona, where he died at age 9. My Sunday school teacher tried to comfort the kids who knew Stevie, by saying that he was in heaven with all of the angels and he was probably showing them how to play baseball, or relaxing up there on a cloud.

Since he had already done the cloud trick, now I thought he would most likely keep a spare halo in a bag in his closet.

Twisted Death Thoughts

I think as a nation we are obsessed with death and near death. The closer I get to it, the more I think about it, and the more I think about the ways it could happen. Certainly the most preferable is dying while sleeping when we turn 120. "It was a complete shock. She seemed so lively, and she looked so young!" However, we are not often afforded the luxury of preference, especially if we have sinned and come short of the glory of God in the week prior to said death. I don't want to die at the hands of someone else or by my own hand; due to disease; in heavy traffic; when there's no one on the road; in the bathroom; doing laundry; after I've paid all my bills; before I've spent all my money; right after I put all the groceries away; during sex; before or after sex; on a cruise ship in the North Atlantic; by lethal injection or electric chair or hanging; by radiation fallout; while I'm working; while I'm on vacation; on my wedding day; right before I get divorced; before my kids grow up; before my grandkids grow up; waiting in line; on an airplane; in a train wreck; on the beach; alone; with my family; freezing; burning; drowning; hit by a baseball I was trying to catch; hit by a baseball I had no idea was coming toward me; falling off of a cliff; slowly; or during a scuffle with a wild animal.

Advertising is full of near-death. Models are heroin-addict thin, even the ones pitching Italian food products. That does not make sense. There is a radio ad about waiting on hold, in which the listener is asked whether he or she would like to be roasted over hot coals rather than wait longer on hold. I guess I'd rather wait. Maybe.

Here is what I want. If I wait on hold for more than 5 to 7 minutes, I get my daughter to come out and wait with me. When the people come back on line, my daughter will scream and speak near the phone. "Oh God, Mom! Mom? (In an agonizing crying voice) Mama is gone! Oh no, she died while waiting for customer service!"

My mother could easily die if we let her watch MTV. She would keel over if she saw what passes for clothing, or respectable hairdos. Never mind the misogynistic, violent attitudes of the artists. Their appearance alone could throw her into a coma.

She comes from Pentecostal folks who used to pass out tracts prohibiting red lipstick at church. "Wear Gloss, Go To Hell." As a teenager, part of my job was to be evil and as sarcastic as possible to my parents. When she was exasperated with my sarcastic mouth, (which I inherited from her) Mom used to tell me that I would be the death of her, and I said, "Unh, uh, because I stepped on two cracks today and your back is just fine."

My sisters just sat back and let me be the evil one, and I developed a kind of shock-antibody from the experience. This was helpful when my own children became teenagers. Quite frankly, it's going to take a lot more than a couple of green mohawks and snarling, half-naked juveniles with guitars to kill me. I figure if my own mirror can't do it, no one else can creep me out that much.

I don't believe I mock death as much as it mocks me. Crows feet, lower back pain, weak bones, tired eyes, fear of large dogs, cancer tests, increased plaque in my veins and on my tooth enamel, these things death has thrown me, "Deal with getting old! Heh, heh, heh."

But I fight back. I watch cartoons, and heartburn be damned, I use Tabasco sauce on everything. And every once in awhile, I tell my mother something like "I've decided to let my daughter go out with a man twice her age, just for the weekend." or "I've decided to become a Hari-Krishna and sell flowers at the Sacramento airport." I figure I am desensitizing her, so that one day, if someone inadvertently turns on MTV in her presence, she could take it. I am single-handedly responsible for the non-death of my mother. Hopefully, my children will continue the tradition.

Chapter 26
TWISTY ANIMALS

Call Kevorkian for Me....

I can't breathe, because I have a cat. They used to say that cats steal the baby's breath, but in my case, it's the adult that wheezes. Allergic reaction. I am allergic to: grass, cats, rabbits, llamas, certain dogs, pollen, dust, lima beans, okra, red grapes, sunflower oil, linseed oil, borax cleanser, bleach, cardboard, clay and paint.

I am probably allergic to chocolate, as well, but I risk it.

My allergies have put me in a bad mood for the last 23 years. So many times I have wondered where the homicidal tendency originates, and I can blame it on the relentless attack of allergies on my respiratory system.

Many times I'll be sitting at my desk thinking of ways to eliminate people who make grammatical mistakes, daydreaming of stabbing poor spellers with poison darts, or clawing the throats of those who use too many words, and I will begin to wheeze and develop a sinus headache.

Allergies have just about ruined my concentration. Who would have thought that twisted murderous thoughts could be interrupted by post-nasal drip? I take generic Actifed and Sudafed and Contac and Tylenol and sinus/allergy tablets and asthma medicine and Pepto-Bismol, and try to assume a degree of normalcy.

I can tell I'm overmedicated when I begin to cry at meetings regarding rice straw issues. I may develop narcolepsy, especially covering local governmental meetings, but I haven't slept longer than 10 seconds yet. Not even when I'm supposed to sleep. I keep waking up wheezing or needing another pill.

The cat watches me sneeze. She looks at me like she's amazed my head has not collapsed. I threaten her with the squirt gun. She goes into the next room to bother the dog. The dog thinks my sneezing is an exciting event. He jumps up and perks up his ears, as though I've just won the lottery.

My co-workers are tired of saying, "Bless you." They say "Blehh...oh, it's just Joie." I tell them to just say it once in the morning and I'm good for the whole day. Sometimes I wonder what that blessing is all about, because the more I get blessed, the more I sneeze.

I talk like Edith Ann, Lily Tomlin's characterization of a 5-year-old. I used to just do an impression, now it's natural, because we both sound lik a participant get for his or her active participation? Some kind of government incentive? Extra nest material? Wal-Mart gift certificates? The press release also states that in 2000, 18 pairs of pandas were "encouraged" to breed. What about the other 134 pandas? Where is their encouragement? Were they bad bears? Do they get any sort of consolation prize? "Please don't breed, and here's a Hershey bar..." I can imagine they'd be on some sort of talk show, if they could...telling Jenny Jones that they were not encouraged by the program, and now survival is just not important to them anymore. "Jenny, I just don't know if I want to be a part of a survival program that only encourages the 'popular' pandas." She would probably have some animal psychiatrist come on the show and explore their feelings. Also, how is breeding an activity that is "encouraged?" The pandas either will or won't, I'd suspect. Most species of animals, including humans, will breed if given the opportunity (and a bottle of wine?). No encouragement is really needed. What do you suppose they did to express this "encouragement?" Did they just say, "Go on, you can do it." I can picture a few cheerleaders standing outside the den, "Be aggressive, B-E-Aggressive!" Or did they take the panda pair to dinner and a movie and expect things to progress naturally? Maybe they stuck the pandas next to the rabbits, although that might b a participant get for his or her active participation? Some kind of government incentive? Extra nest material? Wal-Mart gift certificates?

The press release also states that in 2000, 18 pairs of pandas were "encouraged" to breed. What about the other 134 pandas? Where is their encouragement? Were they bad bears? Do they get any sort of consolation prize? "Please don't breed, and here's a Hershey bar..."

I can imagine they'd be on some sort of talk show, if they could...telling Jenny Jones that they were not encouraged by the program, and now survival is just not important to them anymore. "Jenny, I just don't know if I want to be a part of a survival program that only encourages the 'popular' pandas." She would probably have some animal psychiatrist come on the show and explore their feelings.

Also, how is breeding an activity that is "encouraged?" The pandas either will or won't, I'd suspect. Most species of animals, including humans, will breed if given the opportunity (and a bottle of wine?). No encouragement is really needed.

What do you suppose they did to express this "encouragement?" Did they just say, "Go on, you can do it." I can picture a few cheerleaders standing outside the den, "Be aggressive, B-E-Aggressive!" Or did they take the panda pair to dinner and a movie and expect things to progress naturally? Maybe they stuck the pandas next to the rabbits, although that might be a tad intimidating.

Perhaps they piped in Barry White on the Muzak in the Panda den. Maybe they learned by example..."Ok, we're only going to show you one more time..." Oh, wait. I know. It was more subtle. They had zookeepers walk by the pandas every day, wearing T-shirts that said, "Breeding is Good." Perhaps there were sexually explicit panda films. "Get in there and watch that video," the zookeepers would say encouragingly.

Maybe it was a more rudimentary effort. They put the female in a comfortable "breeding room," all dolled up in panda lingerie (a teddy?), spy cameras in the corner, and place bits of bamboo (a favorite Panda dish) along the path, so that the male panda would be drawn into the room. They say that the quickest way to a man's heart is through his stomach. Perhaps this is also true with Pandas. Of course, they probably didn't want him to have a real heavy meal. That's never good.

Well, whatever they did, it worked. The twin cubs are now out and about, eating bamboo and scampering around, watching all the passersby. The panda parents watch as the twins leave the nesting area to explore, and when the zookeepers aren't watching, they hold paws.

Bird Brained

There are bird meetings going on all around town. Have you seen them? Rows of crows line the telephone wires. I was watching them one day when I was supposed to be writing about a local government meeting, and I think there was some crow talk going on about what to do about Glenn County.

The "meetings" start with three to five birds. More come in later, as though they had a timed item on the agenda. Hmm. Then a couple will fly off, and more will fly in, and there will be a great deal of flapping of wings and a lot of squawking, much like a local government meeting.

After an hour or so, it looks like a decision has been made, and the birds fly away, in search of late worms. Ever since Alfred

Hitchcock's movie, I have been much more aware of our avian friends. I don't want to end up like Tippi Hedren.

Hitchcock was always ahead of his time. What was the real message of "The Birds?" Yeah, they flock together. They do, and we better watch it, pal. Someday when we least expect it, the birds' plan will be revealed. Perhaps it isn't just weird people in Montana who amass weapons. Perhaps the parakeets are planning worldwide domination. Perhaps the loons will retaliate for being called loons.

Perhaps we ought to rethink the whole chicken industry. Are there turkey terrorists? We don't really know. Yet. Because I was a child of the 60s, I am automatically considered a conspiracy theorist, however, I am not the only one who thinks the birds are organized...You saw Chicken Run. I may be more passionate and intense than others. I think there is much more to the animal "kingdom" than meets the eye. I think they really might "have it out for us."

Consider all the animal activists. Who are they trying to appease, hmm? Who gets the benefit of being listed as an endangered species? Not humans, although we endanger ourselves every day. Don't think the government isn't worried about this. The feds have people that go up in planes and count birds. Species with sharp beaks are closely monitored. The birds know they're being watched, so they have to plan very carefully.

The US Fish & Wildlife Service is the federal agency with all the countermeasures for an imminent bird takeover. The agency throws the suspicion off of themselves by calling it the Fish & Wildlife Service. They really care more about the birds than they do the fish. How are you going to worry about fish, anyway? We know where most of them are. With birds, we're not so sure.

Hence, the counting and the building of habitat reserves and the organized bird watching clubs. The wildlife part of the name is so that after the birds make their move, the US Fish & Wildlife people can say, "See? We told you they were wild." It is not so far fetched. Who hasn't approached their parked car and seen bird droppings and heard a sound similar to laughing from a nearby tree? It may be caw, caw, but its really ha, ha.

The plan has been slow in coming, I'll grant you that. It began about 65 million years ago, with the pterodactyls. If they hadn't turned into tar, they would have taken over. Need proof of that? See Jurassic Park III. You probably haven't heard about this before, because people are afraid to talk about it, fearing the birds will find out that we know they're planning something.

Of course, by writing about this, I am putting us all in danger, unless I can guarantee that no one will use this column for cage liner.

How to Kill 'Em...Dead

They are an abomination, and hard to kill. I'm not talking about some mad movie monsters or some tyrannical world leader, but the little slice of insect heaven known as the common cockroach.

These icky bugs are not welcome in my new apartment, yet they insisted on showing up just as we moved in, sort of a welcome to Orland thing. All new Glenn County residents are issued 100,000 roaches per apartment. Why wasn't I informed? The only thing the manager told me was "No pets." Hmm.

They weren't there when I was looking at the apartment; only after I had signed the lease did they invite themselves to join the family. I had to go out at midnight and find two cans of Raid, one for me and one for my daughter. Did you ever see the commercials for Raid in the 60s, when they showed these cute little animated insects being destroyed by this muscle bound can, and the announcer said Raid kills bugs dead? How else can they be killed, I ask you? They can't be killed comatose...But actually, the Raid only half-kills them. Go figure.

Armed with our big red spray cans, we carefully surveyed the area and hunted the beasts down. Upon contact, we sprayed, and they swam, waving their little antennae, kicking around in the pool of Raid. It was a party. We didn't care to join them. We found that if we sprayed them on the wall, they would drop to the ground and then run like heck for the nearest roach opening, so we had to be quick spray and squish, spray and squish.

It also helps to yell and cuss at them while you're squishing. It kind of gives you an inner power, like the yell of a karate master prior to the kick fills him with the power to defeat his opponent. "Die, you damned roach!" The people in the apartment below probably thought I was on the phone.

So here is the picture of the day, a mother and daughter standing back-to-back, armed and dangerous, a twitch in the mother's eye. Both women are looking at the walls and scanning the corners, fingers tapping the nozzles of the cans, muttering "Come on. Make my day." We are ready to shoot.

They are pretty scary to encounter, even though you are much bigger. It's the reputation. Freddie Prinze used to say, "In my building they learned to talk with an accent. They would threaten me when I'd leave, they would say 'Freddie, where are 'ju going? To the grocery store, huh? Don't come back with no roach poison or we'll lock you out." Those were New York roaches.

In Texas, of course, they are much bigger. They wear leather and ride Harleys, carrying handguns. They vote Republican.

Here in Glenn County, they have not developed speech, but there are a lot of antennae waving. I didn't see any motorcycles or election propaganda.

Everyone is so helpful when they hear you have a roach problem. The first thing they say is, "Ew. Gross." or my personal favorite, "Oh, that's too bad." Then they tell you what to buy, since you've already figured out that the roaches are somewhat fond of Raid. They say "Buy the powder stuff, I know it works." The next person you talk to says, "Buy the gel stuff. I know that works." The next person says, "Get those little traps. They work excellently."

So, you buy the powder and the gel and the traps and an extra can of Raid, and suddenly you become confident that this is something you can overcome. I really feel triumphant now. I could march with my fellow roach killers, singing "This little fogger of mine, I'm gonna let it fog" It's a new era in my life, and I'll be darned if I let these little things bug me. I feel like the Scarlett O'Hara of Orland. "I swear it, I'll never be scared again."

Twisty Pet Life

I had a troubled pet life as a child. Every pet I had was quirky, and many met with death a little sooner than expected. Even stranger, I seem to have passed this pet fate along to my children. Their pets have also been sorta weird.

Many of these strange and wonderful pets have a special place in my heart, and now that we have a little terrier saved from the fate of certain death, and named him Kismet, which is Latin for fate, all these cosmic pet ghosts have invaded my dreams.

My first puppy was Sparky, a standard black and white dog, named after the town in which we lived, Sparks, Nevada. (I once read Snoopy was originally going to be called Sparky.)

I was three and a half years old when Sparky was with us. He was an active little puppy, digging holes, burying anything he found. We later dug up several kitchen utensils, as well as doll heads, garden tools, bike parts and a sprinkler head. As Sparky grew, I did not, and soon he was much bigger than me. When I went outside to play with him, he became the Coppertone dog, pulling me around by the seat of my pants. This was fun for Mom to capture on film, but the actual experience was less than thrilling. I wanted a cat.

My first cat was a big gray tabby cat called TC who absolutely loved me and absolutely hated my dad. I was never more than a footstep away from the cat, and most of the time, he did not need to walk. I carried him. From my arms, he growled and scratched at the air when Dad was near. Dad wasn't so fond of TC, either. He would growl back, teasing TC with his cougar imitation. TC ran away.

Next we had a series of cats that Dad said also ran away. One was a little orange and white cat that thought he was a kangaroo. We called him Orange Juice. Rather than walk, he leapt everywhere he went. Mom was constantly coaxing him down from the top of the bookcase or the refrigerator. He once jumped from the floor to the top of the stove. It was on. Bad idea, OJ.

Also in that cat series, we had a kitten that screamed rather than mewed, a six-toed singing mongrel cat, and pure white cat twins who despised human contact.

We had an Alaskan malamute dog that ate everything in his path. He was scary. His name was Wolfie, and he loved smaller animals to death. Then we had Max, a great big black mutt dog, who was friendly, except with Mom. She was scared of him, because we taught him this horrible trick. Whenever we said, "Smile, Max" he would bare his teeth. Poor Mom thought the dog was about to attack her, when he was only smiling. He was actually too old and comfortable to attack anything, but Mom was skeptical.

Mom suggested pet birds, which we had at various times, along with goldfish with short life expectancies, and a hamster who got away the first time we held him. The best bird was a myna bird that recognized the different members of the family, and called us by name. We taught another bird to say "Darn Cat."

When my kids were little, we got five chickens for Easter. We put them in the bottom half of a divided birdcage, with our parakeets and cockatiels in the top. One chicken kept to himself and did not act like the others. As the chickens grew up, we gave the four chicken-ish hens to a friend with a farm. We kept the loner, and named him Doc, because he was like the elf that wanted to be a dentist, instead of just another toy making elf.

Doc graduated from the cage to being a back yard chicken. Our dog, Robbie, looked at him and looked back at us as if to say, "This is one hell of a strange looking dog." Doc modeled after Robbie, lifting his leg on the trees and trying to bark and fetch. He loved for the kids to pet him. The dog thought of his chicken friend as a football, gently swatting him around and watching him fly. Doc sometimes hid from Robbie in the doghouse, which Robbie had refused to occupy.

The last dog we had was Targa, a great little Sharpei. My daughter used to dress her up in various doll outfits and make her model for the family. She actually enjoyed being a super-dog-model. She liked to wear certain hats, but not the bunny ears at Easter time. She also liked to go to Taco Bell. We lived around the corner from a Taco Bell, and if Targa was ever missing from the yard, we knew where to look. We had many talks with Targa, explaining that she had to have money to get a burrito.

So far, Kismet is learning to be one with the family. His quirk? He likes to twirl around and dance on two legs when he hears the Britney Spears CD.

Rooster Rumble

Deep in the night, a conversation that turns one's blood cold..."Ay ay ay, if the creep ain't actin' right, he's gotta be, you know, eliminated."

"No second chances. No matter what the tears."

"So we agree, huh? I take him for a ride tomorrow."

"Yeah. Take him out."

Contrary to what you might think, it isn't Louie and Vinnie discussing a mob hit. Nope, the above is a recent conversation between my Mom and Dad. Yeah, they're in a gang. It is called the Pet Killers. To join this gang you have to live in Texas, and hate all manner of house pets.

You move up in seniority in the gang if you get rid of someone's favorite pet -they call it "icing the hairball." My Dad is way up there in the gang, having arranged the demise of several annoying animals. Pet lovers beware. This man is on the SPCA Most Wanted List.

I have personally witnessed him dancing about the yard with a chainsaw. Dad was about to get rid of the pet rooster; take him for a ride. The chicken belonged to my son, who had taught the bird to be a watchdog. Well, he got too good at his job. The rooster would squawk and peck at all visitors. Mom & Dad were almost afraid to go out and sit on the porch, because the chicken might see them there and think, "Danger." He might fly in the face of that danger, and peck somebody's eyes out. So they came up with the rooster elimination plan.

Don't think of them as arch criminals or evil-minded villains. This is simply the way things work in Texas. If something annoys you, kill it. Actually, you get a count of three. So I wasn't surprised at all when Jack called me and said "Grandpa took the chicken for a ride."

I can just see it. Dad blindfolds the chicken and ties him up. Throws him in the trunk. It's dark outside. Dad throws on his leather jacket, grabs his rifle, jumps in the Toyota and thunders down the back road, on the lookout for cops. In a wooded area, south of town, Dad pops the trunk. He takes the bundled chicken out, places it on the ground. "I'll give you a chance, punk. Go ahead and run."

You think I'm kidding, but I've had 27 cats over the years, and 8 dogs, which have mysteriously disappeared in the middle of the night. Mom and Dad work in tandem in the gang. Mom tells Dad what pets annoy her, and Dad drives them away. They make a good team. They've done it so long now, all Mom has to do is sneeze, and Dad picks up his car keys.

This week, Mom and Dad are taking my granddaughter on a cross-country trip. Ok, she can be as annoying as any 3-year-old, but I think they might be going to an extreme. "Want to go for a ride, Cori?" they asked. All we can do is pray.

Chapter 27
ANTI-GOVERNMENT THOUGHTS

I can hear thousands cheering as I have not written about my family this week. They are glad, too. This week I have decided to bring up several twisted thoughts considered of great importance by OUR government, whom I am reported to trust implicitly.

Actually, my ideal government does not exist. I think the time is right for an angry African-American Jewish woman president with Bill Gates as her running mate. Or maybe we could elect somebody really, really smart, like Dr. Stephen Hawking. Wouldn't that be awesome?

Until something as incredible as that happens, I will continue to make fun of the present government while still respecting the authority they have over me, especially CHP officers who keep me safely and slowly going down the road.

As for laws on the books, I would not dare to call any of them dumb, because someone might interpret me as somewhat cynical. However, I have found a few items in the penal code that could be called, well, weird.

It is against the law to cut a shrubbery. In the Penal Code book, number 384a says you can get arrested and thrown in jail for 6 months and fined up to $1000 for destroying a public shrub. This includes removing leaf mold, unless you are employed to do such removal. I wonder where in California it has become a critical issue that people must be thrown in the pokey for breaking a bush or taking the leaf mold off of a fern.

Was there lobbying for this law, with people picketing? Their signs read "Damn You Plant Pullers!" and "Break a Branch, Go to Jail." Suppose your 5-year-old picks a flower out of the garden at City Hall? "Book 'em Danno."

Here's another weird law, on the books since 1872. Section 598 of the penal code says "Every person who, within any public cemetery or burying ground, kills, wounds, or traps any bird, or destroys any bird's nest other than swallows' nests, or removes any eggs or young birds from any nest, is guilty of a misdemeanor."

What I want to know is WHERE do the swallows go for equal rights? Why are swallows subject to harm without recrimination? And no one knows whether the swallows in question are European swallows or the heavier African swallows. For 127 years, no one has given a -damn about stealing swallows from a cemetery. And suppose a cop caught you taking birds out of a nest at a cemetery. Would they have their guns drawn?

And, how do they know the birds aren't swallows? I can just see it. The cops yell from behind their car door, via megaphone..."Put the chicks back, man. Don't make us hurt you, pal."

"But they're swallows, officer."

"Oh. Ok. Carry on, then."

And what would you be doing in a cemetery removing birds in the first place, swallows or not? Is it avant garde? Can you see the commercials? "I do all my bird stealing at Smith Cemetery. They have the best nests in town."

Section 638a says it is unlawful for any person to implant foreign materials within the scalp of another person for the purpose of alleviating baldness, unless that person is licensed to do so. My problem with this law is that it makes so much sense. It also means that more than one person must have tried it without a license, which means that people are running around with illegal hair.

Jail time and up to a $5000 fine is the punishment for importing into California for commercial purposes (or possession with intent to sell) the dead body of an alligator, crocodile, polar bear, leopard, ocelot, tiger, cheetah, jaguar, sable antelope, wolf, zebra, whale, cobra, python, sea turtle, colobus monkey, kangaroo, vicuna, sea otter, free-roaming feral horse, dolphin, porpoise, Spanish lynx or elephant. Ok.

If you have any dead vicunas (which is, as you know, a South American mammal similar to a llama, with fine silky fleece) lying around the house, don't sell them. I get it. The law is not complicated. But tell me how a feral horse can be free-roaming if it's dead. I think you'd have to change that to non-roaming. And it wasn't so free roaming when it was alive, if you caught it.

If you have a dead elephant, your neighbor is likely to turn you in. It's not easy to hide those pachyderms. Of course, you can say you weren't going to sell it, but I think the FBI would see right through that. And, once again, the swallows are not protected. Not even dead ones. If you're not on the list, you ain't get tin' on the ark, bud.

If you buy a soda out of a vending machine and it steals your money, you have no right to kick it. The machine has more rights than you, Mr. Orwell. It is a misdemeanor to beat a vending machine. Actually, the law is that you can't cheat a vending machine by putting in slugs. But they sure have the right to cheat you.

Tired of the Penal Code, I moved on to more light reading. In the American Heritage Dictionary, you can see a picture of a glockenspiel as well as a picture of a couple of gnus on the same page. Ok. I can understand these illustrations, but why is there a picture of a rug near the definition of a rug? Isn't it perfectly clear what a rug might look like when you read "A piece of heavy fabric used to cover a floor"? Are we really not familiar with the concept?

I'm moving on to review other books; be on the lookout for controversy regarding the Betty Crocker Cookbook.

Positive Steps—Watch Where You're Stepping
Recent legislation was proposed to start calling pet owners "Pet Guardians" so that a stigma would not be attached to your pooch, and he wouldn't feel like he was "owned." One of the proponents of the legislation likened "ownership" of PETS to slavery. Slavery!

How could a furry little animal that never listens to you ever be considered a slave? Like you make your dog pick cotton. Uh, huh. Like your gerbil calls you Master. Listen. If I bought a Sharpei for $650, I own the puppy. I didn't become his guardian.

These poor pets. With this new legislation, I am sure you'll start to see them by the hundreds lining up at the courthouse, ready to sue the pants off of their "guardians." Like your dog tells other dogs, "That guy who gives me Kibbles and Bits wants to call me Tobey. I'm going to sue him, and then I'm going to bite the cat."

Unfortunately, they are not allowed in the courthouse, unless they are seeing-eye dogs, and even then, how many seeing-eye dogs represent other animals in court? None. They are slaving away, keeping blind people from obstruction. So who will speak for them? Why it's the Animal Activists! The people who appreciate animals better than people. Worst kind of person on earth? An animal activist who is also a lawyer.

I say leave the lab rats alone. Let them be lab rats. They don't know from sewer to lab. Let the spotted owls and their would-be saviors live together in peace and harmony in the savior's backyard.

I do think we should stop hunting whales altogether. Hunting any animal to extinction is illogical. Lab rats, on the other hand, are not anywhere close to becoming extinct. You can test my make-up on them. Paint them up like Dennis Rodman for all I care. Is that torture?

Now there is Resolution 189, the Shark Finning Resolution. Apparently there is a huge market for shark fins, and particularly cruel people will go out and slice off a shark's fins and discard the carcass.

A recent press release from a Congressman said this practice is responsible for a growing number of senseless shark deaths, with more than 60,000 sharks killed in 1998.

Ok, first of all, there is already a federal law against finning. Yet legislators voted recently to have Pacific fisheries put an end to the "cruel torture of sharks" by passing this resolution. That ought to work. Congressmen think this is a "positive step" toward protecting the poor sharks.

Second, Hello, these are sharks we're talking about. Sharks. With huge nasty JAWS that bite PEOPLE and swallow them. There were movies about this in the 70's. Talk to Roy Scheider. There was even one in 3-D, to make sure the message got across -Sharks Bad...People Swim Too Slow.

Isn't all death senseless? Why should 60,000 sharks be lionized in death when there are just as many raccoons that become road kill? Actually, shark meat is rather tasty. It's too bad the carcasses are wasted. Why don't they sell the carcasses for meat products, and then there won't be a problem if someone takes the fins.

It would be more like organ donation for animals. They could fill out little cards at the DMV, if they were allowed to go in. And they would be allowed to go in, if they were seeing-eye sharks. I'm sorry if I'm a little insensitive to the pain of de-finned sharks. Maybe the sharks need guardians. I would certainly never own one.

Musical Conspiracy

The government continues to conspire against the people. "They" are in the music, as they have been for many years. Some secret office in Washington, D.C. has a panel of men deciding the fate of our ears -I just know it.

I only bring this up because I think we're all a little tired of shameless promotion. Repetition makes us crazy, because of the neuro-transponders. The "panel" gathers their kazoos and accordions and banjos and makes up a popular song, pays off some "song writer," then they scientifically inject these transponders into the song, and then they direct the Federal Communications Commission to play the song every 20 seconds on our radios.

This allows the government to gather information from our brainwaves as well as transmit subliminal messages such as "Buy American" or "Vote Democratic" or "Drink Budweiser." Currently, the most annoying song on the planet is "Mambo #5," and the video is just as bad, with barely clad girls shaking their parts in time to the mindless accordion-sounding semi-reggae beat, while the singer rhymes about all the different girls that he needs to be near in a 24-hour period.

He is dressed like a pimp from a 1970s detective show and what really worries me is that the first four mambos weren't good enough to be played as much as #5. What could their messages have been? # 5's message is obviously that fedoras are "in."

Last summer, the song heard every 20 seconds was "Wild, Wild West" by Wil Smith. At first, it was to promote the movie, and then it was simply to raise our blood pressure to a "wicky, wicky, wild" level. The video included many thousand tarantulas, which is always good, but there were no tarantulas in the movie. The government wants us to fear only music video tarantulas.

Before that, we all started to wish Celine Dion's heart would not go on, but should stop before she sings that song again. I hate to think of the Titanic and hear Celine Dion. I wonder what the message was from Washington, because I didn't get it, even subliminally.

The "panel" is powerful. Think about any song you've ever heard on a kazoo (an instrument of the government) and suddenly, you're in Tower Records buying a CD of "The Macarena." Government influence is the only way to explain the popularity of "The Macarena."

This is not new. Remember other songs that were played to death on the radio? "Fame" by Irene Cara, "You Light Up My Life" by Debbie Boone, anything by Olivia Newton-John, "I Am Woman" by Helen Reddy, and everything ever done by the Bee Gees, Milli Vanilli or the Chipmunks. People all over America have run from the room when they hear these intensely popular songs—"You Light Up My Life" was the Prom Theme for my graduating class, and the song played at every wedding in 1977.

The Chipmunks recorded a remake of the Billy Ray Cyrus song, "Achy Breaky Heart" which was repeated on the airwaves more than 37 billion times in the original version. When the average person gets a song like that stuck in his or her head, he or she needs to be around people who do not have weapons. Need I say more?

We won't get into the gritty details, I will just tell you that country music was started by one of the members of the panel who wanted people to join the NRA, shop at Wal-Mart and visit Branson, Missouri. Prior to governmental intervention, Branson lounges did not exist, and no one ever had a desire to go to Missouri.

Sadly, even Christmas has had its seasonal beauty disrupted by the U.S. Government. Think about "The 12 Days of Christmas." Before the "panel" came up with that one, there was only one day of Christmas, and it wasn't associated with the purchase of several birds. I don't know where they were going with that, anyway. Birds are still not a traditional Christmas gift, no matter how many times you've sung along regarding geese a-laying and partridges in pear trees. An inordinate amount of birds in any one song should make one suspicious of the government, shouldn't it?

"Do You Hear What I Hear?" That one scrapes my soul. I just want to yell, "Yes! Dammit. I Hear What You Hear, I am in the same room." I used to have a faulty transmitter as a child, I'm sure. Because I used to get the words wrong or the meaning was unclear. In "I Saw Mommy Kissing Santa Claus" I heard ""she thought that I was stuffed up in my bedroom fast asleep." In reality, the girl was "tucked up."

Where is Orientar? Haven't you heard about "We Three Kings of Orientar?" And what about that little drummer boy? When I was little, I thought Jesus' name was "Parumpapumpum."

"I have no gift to bring Parumpapumpum, that's fit to give our King, Parumpapumpumrumpapumpumrumpapumpum, (his full name)" Was it childish confusion or governmental subterfuge?

The only truly unblemished great Christmas song is "Jingle Bells." It cannot be played badly, Even on kazoo, accordion or banjo. It must have been written by an anti- governmental revolutionary. I used to sing "Jingle Bells" when I did not know the words to the hymns in church. Everybody else was singing "Bringing In The Sheaves" and I bopped along in a one-horse sleigh.

Singing "Jingle Bells" can help people come out of deep depression at any time of year. There is a scene in the Charlie Brown Christmas special, where Lucy tries to get Schroeder to play Jingle Bells, and he plays it in several styles including Beethoven, jazz, and Wurlitzer -she keeps asking for the traditional song -and his final rendition is the sound of a toy piano, And she yells, "That's It!" A truly happy tune, no Official Skullduggery. You know what's next. You're going to want to party like it's 1999, but is it really YOUR idea or did the artist formerly known as Prince write that after a visit to Washington?

Acronym City...

We live in a world of acronyms. Everything is abbreviated. Every day life is full of initials. If you're unemployed and need help, you go to HRA, give them your SSI number and your CDL number and all sorts of other numbers.

Your children go to WIS or WHS. There, they decide whether to join the NRA or the NBA. In charge of the county schools is GCOE. You go to meetings of the WUSD, where they tell you about WUTA or API or KTEA.

Then you go out to dinner at KFC. The next day there is trouble involving the CHP, WPD and GCSO. You're afraid they might call in the FBI or the CIA. Cops have their own acronyms! They say UTL or

NFA when they don't do anything. Of course, when they do take action, it is usually about a DUI or A&B.

An election was recently held involving the GCEA and UPEC. If you want money, you go to the ATM at B of A, unless you have NSF, then you suffer, or borrow from MOM. You use a VHS tape in your VCR. That way you can see a movie called ET or MIB or U571. If you have cable you can watch HBO. If you've watched your entire collection of Disney tapes, you can hop in your SUV and drive to AMH and rent T2.

Be careful when you drive or you may end up exceeding the MPH and receive a TKT, lose your CDL and have to deal with the DMV. Don't get busted for a DUI when you have children in DARE or FNL. Not to mention MADD. Just drink your JD at home. But don't spill on your PC.

Of all those who suffer from acronimity, it must be city and county officials who suffer most. Name a County Supervisor who doesn't use all of the following acronyms on a daily basis. RCAC, RCD, RC&D, AT&T, CBDD, CLOC, GCID, REF, AAA, PG&E, GMC, GCFB, HMO, USF&W, F&G, DWA, SACA, FWA, RGI, WIB, CSAC, HSA, DOJ, GCAC, JFK, L&M, JPA, WWII, CalFed, CalTrans, CalOSHA, NorCal, and CalWorks.

This is completely exclusive of the enormous amount of "dot-comming" we all do daily. In your personal life, acronyms have become second nature. Don't believe me? Do you try to avoid MSG and high LDL cholesterol? In this way, you might lose LBS, unless you have no thin gene in your DNA.

Do you use a roll-on to avoid spraying CFCs into the atmosphere? Do you fly? It's controlled by the FAA. Do you listen to the radio? It's controlled by the FCC. Do you go to church? Is it LDS or A of G? Have you ever done drugs? Do you have enough LSD and THC in your system?

Here at the paper, we have our own acronyms, but mostly we strive to win a yearly CNPA award. What will my next column be about? Well, that's TBA.

Twisted Ticket

I almost became an unlicensed writer. I must confess I violated the law of this County and the State of California. I sped. I got caught. I got ticketed. I procrastinated about paying. I got painfully reminded.

So I've been driving very carefully, holding my breath. Then I got a chance to tell it to the judge. Early Monday morning, the sky was bright blue and the sun shone on the courthouse as violators lined up to see the Judge about their tickets. The line was out the door and down the steps of the courthouse. There was some nervous chatter, but no one was too cheerful.

The Courthouse cop asked, "Is there anyone in line with a pocket knife or other weapon?" No one jumped up to say "Me, I have one," so he went back to his desk. After checking in with the court clerk, the perpetrators filed upstairs to await their judgment in the courtroom, where there was no oxygen.

Everyone took a big breath of air before going in. A heavy pall of depression hung over the courtroom; much like a black rain cloud. The wait for the judge was 40 minutes, during which time several people were reviewing their lives and crossing themselves. The movie of my life isn't 40 minutes long, so I had extra time to worry.

My life flashing before my eyes is more like four minutes, one decade per minute. When it was over, I just sat and thought, "Well, that sucked." Finally, the judge was there, and he called the names of several people who weren't there. I thought they must have evaporated due to lack of oxygen. You know they'll be there the next time they're called, oh and they'll be wearing orange.

The judge explained that we, the violators, could plead guilty, not guilty, no contest, or guilty with an explanation, and it better be a really good explanation. Apparently there is no good explanation for exceeding 100 miles per hour in Glenn County. There were several cases of folks driving that fast, but they probably won't do it again. It is costly.

I was there because I got a ticket two years ago that I never paid, because I had other tremendous bills. Tremendous. Big bills. Enormous bills. Bills you don't want to believe. Way big bills. Bills that weighed a ton. Anyway, then I got a notice that I was in big trouble. So I went in to make a payment and they told me it was too late. Five minutes too late. I was already in the computer and I was in big trouble, and all I could do was beg for mercy from the judge.

Here's some logic. If you don't have the money to pay your fine, you are charged EVEN MORE. If you still can't pay, then they can take away your license and you can't go to work to make money to pay. Justice is not only blind; she's a little retarded. Anyway, I told the judge the story of my finances. It took 30 seconds. He was looking over my papers, and I was ready to cry and beg MERCY, PLEASE!

All of a sudden he reduced my fine and said I was ok to drive again, and I had to restrain myself from jumping up and down and screaming with excitement like a contestant on The Price Is Right. Instead I just said "Thank you, sir." And this big beam of light came into the courtroom and there was this voice from heaven that said, "Last chance. Don't mess up again."

When I got out the court door, I went "Yea!" fairly loud, and I nearly slid down the banister, but I thought I might fall on my behind. It felt like Monopoly, when you get the Community Chest card that says the bank made an error in your favor and you get to keep your money and you use it to put a hotel on Boardwalk and then someone who has been mean to you lands on Boardwalk and you do the "I'm putting you into bankruptcy" dance all around the table and everyone says "Settle down, sister."

Woo hoo! I didn't have to go directly to jail without passing Go. I lived to circle the board again. Unfortunately, I am down to the last couple of pink fives.

Legislation Blues

Frankly, I am worried about the future. There are too many little bitty rules now. Rules that affect my well being. I hereby protest the legislation of sweet & sour sauce. This is a conspiracy to drive us all nuts.

McDonalds has a regulation regarding how many packets of sauce are appropriate for so many McNuggets. If you order four to six McNuggets, you get one sauce packet. That's it. No more, unless you pay the sauce fee of eleven cents per packet. Not a dime, but eleven cents.

If you order nine McNuggets, you may have two sauce packets for free. For 20 McNuggets, you may have four sauce packets. If you order extra sauce at the drive-up window, the cashier takes more than a casual glance at your license plate. Suppose you want more than one kind of sauce? This is also frowned upon by McDonalds officials. How dare you want Hot Mustard AND Barbecue sauce!

There is no such regulation regarding Taco Bell hot sauce. You can have as much hot sauce as you desire. (Save it for your McNuggets.) Some guy I know had enough hot sauce packets to give all the neighborhood children two packets in their Halloween bags. I don't suppose it went over too well with all the candy, but at least there was variety. Non-regulated variety.

Frowners are everywhere when you decide to take advantage of free stuff. If you walk around the produce section of the grocery store and you take more than one plastic bag, watch out. Take a bag, put in your bell pepper, and take an extra bag. Put it in your hip pocket, with part of it sticking out. See if they don't stop you at the check stand.

If you're reading a magazine at the dentist's office and you have to wait an extra long time for him to inflict his brand of pain, I say take all the magazines home. Even the ones no one reads. You're at a law office, and there's a candy dish full of Hershey's kisses just sitting there on the desk. Dump them all in your pocket. It may be the only sweetness you get out of a lawyer. The bank pen isn't attached -it's yours. If it is attached to their desk, tell them it is out of ink. They'll give you another one, not attached. Keep it.

If you see a sign that says keep off the grass, keep off of it until the very last step, then jump up and down on it for a few seconds. No one will arrest you. This is what I call revenge of the little man against big government. Break tiny rules, not big ones.

The more restrictions imposed on the sauce packet-loving crowd, the more we should rebel in little ways. Pay parking tickets in pennies. Wash your entire car at the gas station with the window squeegie. Take your time. If anyone gives you grief, say in a gruff way, "This is my revenge against THE MAN!" Revert back to your third grade self. After a day full of meetings, when you're saying the Pledge of Allegiance for the fourth time in one day, say "invisible" instead of "indivisible." It will make you smile.

Modernization. A Good Thing?

Prior to February of 1913, the Internal Revenue Service, or U.S. Bureau of Revenue, as it was known then, accepted live chickens as tax payments. Until 1913 rolled around, livestock meant something to the U.S. Government. Then modernization poked its ugly head into the picture.

Of course, there was an initial protest. Farmers throughout America called the new law unfair. The government prevailed, however, insisting on hard currency or bank-check only methods of payment. They said currency was much less apt to die in transit.

Chickens certainly lost the battle, becoming much less popular, except as Sunday dinner. But it may have been a good thing, in the long run, as it would be hard to stuff a chicken in an ATM. Imagine paying for merchandise at Wal-Mart with chickens. "That will be $25.47, or 12 and a half chickens."

"Oh, God. I only have 9 chickens and 3 eggs. I'll have to put back the beer."

And what about vending machines? The slots would have to be made much bigger. How about taking live chickens to the grocery store? Would it be convenient to buy a dead, frozen chicken for the price of a live chicken? Imagine the clucking as you traverse the frozen food aisle. The shape of wallets would be different, hmm? And one would speculate as to whether one species of chicken would be worth more than another...

If someone came to your yard and killed your chickens, would it be a burglary or murder? Chicken security would get beefed up, wouldn't it? Would people stop eating the incredible edible egg? Would kids stop egging houses on Halloween? On the other hand, what if a thief tried to rob you? "Gimme all your chickens, man." Just hand them over. It's not worth losing your life over a chicken or two.

Modernization shocked Americans even before 1913, when there was scandal over the 1906 bathing suits that naughtily revealed the woman's arms, necks and calves. How dare a woman not wear shoes and gloves on the beach?

Several men were offended by the impure visage of the woolen bathing suits that barely covered the women's knees, and exposed their throats to sunlight. Swimwear is just as shocking today, apparently, because there are women in Florida who were arrested last year for wearing thong bikinis at the beach, without full derriere coverage.

Imagine the 1913 men at the 1999 beach, where a string is acceptable body covering. Imagine them at the nude beaches. They would tell us that modernization is taking us straight to H-E-double toothpicks.

The latest incidence of modernization creeping up on us is the name change of 20th Century Insurance to 21st Century Insurance, not worth mentioning in and of itself, except that they didn't bother to change the name until the first week of January, 2000. No one heard a peep out of them during December. And you'd think they'd have heard about the new century as far back as October. But no, now that it's February, their campaign to leap into modern life is in full swing and they want everyone to know they've changed their name to keep up with the times.

It seems odd, because you know they had to have their

computers in compliance with Y2K, so why not change the name about the same time? It didn't occur to them that the new century would impact their name? I think it was someone named Ralph in accounting, who sent a memo to his boss, saying "Oh, guess what? I heard on the radio that the new century is coming up. It might be a good idea to change our name, to appeal to the folks living in the next century." But nobody listened to Ralph's newfangled, modern idea, until January, that is.

How to Win an Election...

All these candidates for office are giving us their propaganda; I mean platforms, so I thought I would help them out with their speeches.

I think it's important to start out with something like "I'm running for this office because I heard they don't do random drug testing." Or, "As a Trustee, I can be trusted." Then the honesty should play in..."The pay is really good, more than I made last year, for sure."

Or go for total honesty..."My friend, so and so, is on the Board, so they said I should be on it, too, and then we can go out to lunch a lot." For yard signs, I think a good slogan is "You wouldn't want to give me a job as Supervisor, would you?" or "If you vote for me, I'll be your best friend." Another good one is "I have only been in jail twice. And it wasn't my fault. Vote for me."

For television ads, it could be as simple as "Vote for me, 'cause the other guy sucks." Maybe a more aesthetic approach would be a video of a little girl running through a meadow, sort of like the Little House on the Prairie opener, and a voice-over saying "This little girl is happy because her parents are going to vote for me."

If called upon to speak to an important cause, a candidate should say "There is nothing more important to me than the issues. The issues mean a lot. Let me just stress the importance of the issues, because I am very concerned about them. Whoo, boy, are the issues meaningful! What issues am I speaking of, you ask? Well, the ones that are so important to me and to you."

In an open debate, a candidate should have a stray lock of hair waving around out of place, so that no one pays attention to what they are saying. If the candidate is hair- impaired, they should remember to use the word "paradigm" in every other sentence.

When the other candidates speak, our candidate should cough or sneeze while saying the word "Horse feathers." If a question throws the candidate for a loop, he should look wildly around the room, as though someone moved his water dish, and draw in a big-breath, saying "I think some of you in the audience must be communists!"

When talking about himself, the candidate should always say he is happily married and his children went to Ivy League schools. Never mind the facial twitch that accompanies such a statement. He is a long-time resident and loving family man. You bet he is. Really.

Of course, the only way to really win is to have the most hair and the best toothy grin (Carry a mirror to check for spinach on the teeth). Winking and giving a "thumbs up" sign is also acceptable if done sparingly and at the appropriate times. Now go out there and win!

If We Only Had A Brain...

Okay, here's the thing. The people in Washington D.C. believe the people in Florida. The rest of us know how dumb it all sounds not to be able to follow an arrow to a nearby hole, but bureaucrats actually think Palm Beach County residents had trouble with the concept. "The ballot was confusing," said a Florida blonde. "Oh dear," said the government.

This is exactly why the government funds studies on how worms mate, and why water flows downhill. It is our fault. We the people, especially people in Florida, have acted so irresponsible and stupid that the government thinks a majority of us are irresponsible and stupid. And we keep proving them right.

THE VANILLA PEOPLE

Television has not helped, lately. We are all addicted to Who Wants To Be A Millionaire. Yet, some people miss the stupidest questions. I used to be offended that they asked those stupid questions like -What color is the sky? A) Red; B) Blue; C) Black; or D) Magenta with gray stripes. Now, I think if someone from Palm Beach, Fla. were sitting there in front of Regis Philbin, they might have to phone a friend for the answer.

A new late night show is called "Street Smarts." The host finds three people, late at night, who have likely had too much celebration in liquid form, and asks each one a fairly easy question, nothing on the scale of Jeopardy, but "Who is the Secretary of State?" or "Whom would you call if you had a clogged aorta?" Then the host has two people from the audience vote on whether or not the contestants will answer properly.

Of course, two of the three contestants answer "Mom" to both questions. The third may or may not get it right. The play continues with total strangers voting on the stupidity of other strangers. Watching these shows has lowered my confidence in the national IQ. That's intelligence quotient.

Where are all the smart people hiding? Ok, I know, it's not fair to look at TV or Florida and make a -generalization about the rest of us. But "they" do think of us as dumb consumers. Read on. Here's the latest Public Service Announcement. Hmm. Participants are needed for a "miracle" weight loss study out of guess where, Washington D.C.

A 5-year study will determine whether Japanese fat-reducing rings (worn on the fingers) will be effective. The makers of the rings claim that wearing it on the thumb reduces fat in the face, on the second finger -in the arms, the middle finger -in the stomach, on the fourth finger -the waist, the pinkie finger -the thighs. Selected participants will be paid up to $250 to report their weight and food intake to the Fat Reduction Institute.

Here's the unbelievable part. The Institute hopes that consumers will be able to tell the difference between fact and fiction when it comes to advertising claims. So, within five years, the people in Washington, D.C. hope that we, the people, will smarten up. I think it will depend on the election results, which, hopefully will be finalized within those same five years.

Winning Strategies—Decision 2000

It's mud-slinging time, as the primaries edge nearer, nearer. In Glenn County, the races for Board of Supervisor and Willows Unified School District Governing Board have not generated a glob of mud flung at anyone, so it's a given that the voter turnout will be low.

We believe that the only mud slinging allowed will be those running unopposed.

Now just because the candidates are behaving doesn't mean we can't enjoy a truckload of propaganda. Take a look at the Propositions. There are some from the last campaign, just wrapped up in a different package, and there are those propositions or props as they are known in the "biz," that are totally bogus because there is already a similar law on the books, and there are the bond issues that will generate money for everyone in California, except for where you live.

Then there's the world of education. It is time for a little change in ethics, folks. Have you heard the plagiarized commercial for Proposition 26? We hear a man and a woman arguing, "More accountability!" "Reduced class size!" Then a third party, with an obviously cooler head tells the two, "You don't have to choose." Apparently Proposition 26 allows for the happiness of all. The last line is "Proposition 26. It's all you ever wanted in a proposition, and more."

Tell me you haven't heard it before and I will remind you of the classic beer commercial which has been adapted for education. "Great taste!" "Less filling!" Argue, argue, argue; cool-headed guy enters. "Hey, you don't have to choose. Drink this."

"Wow! It is all you ever wanted in a beer and more." Does

Proposition 26 make you want a beer? How about your children? Because campaign strategists lifted the general idea and adapted their script, does it make them clever? Are they ethical?

Does the world of educators approve of the beer commercial tactic? Or are we just ignorant enough to accept the words they stuff into our ears as gospel from the Almighty legislature? Are all the propositions a true reflection of the issues the people want to address?

Let us consider Proposition 23. This is the "None of the above" ballot option, which would allow voters to select "none of the above" rather than a named candidate. "None of the above" votes will be tallied, but only votes for named candidates will count for purposes of determining election results. Hello. Here's an option, but it won't count. Oh, where do I sign up? I would love to have that option of knowing my vote doesn't count. If this makes sense to you, please call and explain it to me in simple words.

I urge you to vote in March for the candidate of your choice then go find something that tastes great but is less filling and celebrate the primaries in style.

When You Gotta Go...

Another rule has reared its ugly head, this time at the schools. I am told it is not really a rule it is a "procedure." It is a strange one indeed, and has to do with the flow of, well let's say creativity.

A student may not use the restroom during class time more than one time per class per grading period. To violate this rule means the student must make up time after school. Go potty, Get detention.

Doesn't that ruin the training I did as the parent of a toddler years ago? Who is going to pay for that child's therapy? Whose valuable class time is really wasted? (Last time I checked, they don't wait until you come back to continue the lesson plan.)

What is the alternative and how would THAT waste time??? Oh, I get the thinking behind it. Students should use the bathroom on their own time during the few minutes they get to go to the next class, which is across campus, after they drop off books in their locker. Or wait until lunchtime, or heck, you have a bathroom at home. You should have thought of it before you left.

I am told I am making a big deal of this. A student could, on any given day, legally visit the rest room 15 times. The next day, however, he or she would be restricted to before and after school, between classes and lunchtime, 8 times. Eight visits may seem like a lot to you, even if you don't have teenagers. But even if you had 7 more legal chances, sometimes you gotta go and you can't wait. Why legislate it?

Last year, apparently there were hundreds of teens abusing the potty privilege, asking to use the facilities with reckless abandon. It's the same people trying to get away with it, over and over, which, to me, sounds like there's a solution within the stated problem.

I wonder how they came up with the current "solution" to curb the urge to use the hall pass. One person who enjoys the daily thrill of inspiring scholars to think great thoughts would suggest a hall pass policy. Maybe another lover of education's solution would be a referral to a urologist. Maybe another quality-minded thinker would suggest that- the habitual visitation is really a cry for help and the offenders should be counseled intensively.

Maybe the solution should be better bathroom monitoring. Make sure whoever is going is really going. Oh, no, wait. That might be a violation of civil rights. Crap. Well they had to come up with something. The potty problem was more than petty. Let's not worry about school shootings. Let's take care of the big issues. Imagine the headlines...Crowds of Incontinent Classmates Conspire to Cut Chemistry...Teachers Take Toilet- Trained Teens To Task...Sink or Stink, Say Seniors...Filthy Freshmen Found Flunking French...Don't Do It During Dodge Ball...

Now the bladders of the underclassmen are paying for last year's tomfoolery. Hold it. I cannot think of anything I could possibly learn in the three minutes it would take to go use the restroom that would be of more importance than the thought that I might have an embarrassing episode if I wait.

Here is where the government has too much influence over education, folks. It's not Ritalin. It's toilet paper. Let's educate our young 'uns to believe those who make the rules can govern our bodily functions. Making too much of this, HAH! How far we have come from the Revolutionary War, when the battle cry was "Give me liberty or give me death." Now it's "Give me a hall pass or I will wet my drawers."

You would think that a fine institution of higher learning, which produces a great number of outstanding college bound honor students, would not make their classrooms feel like prison camp. They ought to have a "procedure" to allow for the "elimination" of this urination probation.

Monica Schmonica

Warning: The following column may contain the word "sex" or "sex act" or and may be referred to as "did it." I also use the word "cigar" in an unnatural setting. This may offend some folks, so don't read this out loud by the water cooler like you usually do.

Monica Lewinsky was not famous. She was infamous. Profiting from infamy is popular these days. So, Jenny Craig hopped on the Lewinsky bandwagon and decided to pay the infamous former intern a bundle of bucks to drop some fat and be an advertisement for how well the Jenny Craig system works.

The horrendous amount of money ($50,000 per pound) will be handed over to a thinner, and more popular Monica upon completion of the process. Ok. I have some problems with this.

1. I do not care how much Monica weighs. Apparently, neither did Clinton.

2. Why does the Jenny Craig fan club want a thinner Monica? Is there something wrong with the image of a fat girl who "did it" with the President? Would our perception of Monica change if she were thinner? Are we supposed to revere her now and emulate her behavior once she drops four or five dress sizes? Why is she such a wonderful card to draw? Is it her influence over other young fat

girls who want to have sex with a married man? Or maybe it is her ability to get away with sex acts with a world leader without any public scorn.

3. Wouldn't a more economic endeavor be for someone to sell T-Shirts with a picture of Monica with a cute little saying ballooning out of her mouth, like "Show me your cigar" or "Got a Havana?" This would be a new way for tobacco companies to profit, as well. The t-shirts could be the wrappers for individual cigars. How about an advertising campaign for a dry-cleaner using Monica's image? They could say "We remove stains from blue dresses all the time." And Monica could endorse them with a big wink and a "thumbs up" gesture. Or perhaps she could be the spokesperson for Trojan, and the ad could be her placing a condom over a helium dispenser and then ingesting the helium, and saying, "All my men wear Trojans, or they wear nothing at all." The helium voice would truly sell the product, don't you think?

4. Anyone else wishing to lose a great deal of weight must pay Jenny Craig an enormous amount of money. This is the essence of free enterprise. Buy my weight loss method, and I guarantee you'll get thinner, because you'll owe me so much money you won't be able to afford to eat. When "the system" is backwards, it ceases to be an incentive for the rest of us.

For instance, who wouldn't eat cardboard to get $50,000 per lost pound? I would pledge to lose 500 pounds. Why doesn't Jenny Craig contact me? I could be just as influential to Jenny's other customers as Monica, even though I've never met a man from Arkansas worth "doing." I have been an intern, but I do not own a stained blue dress.

While we're on this, I don't care how much the Duchess of York weighs, either. Sarah

Ferguson probably makes millions of dollars for Weight Watchers when she can afford any method of weight loss. Yeah, I believe she eats out of Weight Watcher cartons. Sure. And I have a gland problem.

Next there will be a more realistic campaign for weight loss, with the Taco Bell dog saying, "I used to be a Great Dane. Then I met Jenny Craig."

ONE LAST TWISTED THOUGHT

Grandma Savage once told me I had something special inside me. I think it was this book. (And maybe a sequel.)
Thank you Grandma!

THE END